Academic Writing and Grammar for Students

Education at SAGE

SAGE is a leading international publisher of journals, books, and electronic media for academic, educational, and professional markets.

Our education publishing includes:

- accessible and comprehensive texts for aspiring education professionals and practitioners looking to further their careers through continuing professional development

- inspirational advice and guidance for the classroom

- authoritative state of the art reference from the leading authors in the field

Find out more at: **www.sagepub.co.uk/education**

SAGE Study Skills

Academic Writing and Grammar for Students

Alex Osmond

Los Angeles | London | New Delhi
Singapore | Washington DC

Los Angeles | London | New Delhi
Singapore | Washington DC

SAGE Publications Ltd
1 Oliver's Yard
55 City Road
London EC1Y 1SP

SAGE Publications Inc.
2455 Teller Road
Thousand Oaks, California 91320

SAGE Publications India Pvt Ltd
B 1/I 1 Mohan Cooperative Industrial Area
Mathura Road
New Delhi 110 044

SAGE Publications Asia-Pacific Pte Ltd
3 Church Street
#10-04 Samsung Hub
Singapore 049483

Editor: Marianne Lagrange
Editorial assistant: Kathryn Bromwich
Project manager/proofreader: Sharon Cawood
Assistant production editor: Thea Watson
Copyeditor: Rosemary Campbell
Marketing manager: Catherine Slinn
Cover designer: Wendy Scott
Typeset by: C&M Digitals (P) Ltd, Chennai, India
Printed by Ashford Colour Press Ltd

Library of Congress Control Number: 2012935990

British Library Cataloguing in Publication data

A catalogue record for this book is available from the British Library

ISBN 978-1-4462-1090-1
ISBN 978-1-4462-1091-8 (pbk)

MIX
Paper from
responsible sources
FSC
www.fsc.org   FSC® C011748

Contents

About the Author

Photo credit: Oliver Wright

Alex Osmond has worked as an Academic Skills Adviser, helping to launch Brunel University's ever-expanding ASK service, and is now VLE Project Manager at the university. As part of these roles, he has provided guidance to students both online and face-to-face, focusing on the development of their academic writing. Students have been consistent in praising the advice he has given, which has often translated directly into higher grades. Alex has also taught a wide variety of skills sessions across Brunel's degree programmes. He has worked to develop online resources aimed at improving academic writing, and also co-managed the Study Skills Collection at Brunel University Library. Before working at Brunel, Alex worked at the University of Wales Institute, Cardiff, as an Academic Skills Adviser. A key role here was the design of a comprehensive suite of online lessons to help first-year students reflect on second-year module choices. The module this was a part of was nominated for a Times Higher Award in Outstanding Student Support. Alex has focused on the English language in his studies and work for several years, and his approach highlights the importance of independent learning in students developing a well-rounded set of skills.

Acknowledgements

Many people were involved in putting this book together, contributing ideas, and generally helping me through the daunting experience of writing and publishing a first book. I'll admit that I hope it gets easier, but at the same time, it's been a very positive experience!

The team at SAGE made this experience much less stressful than it could have been, and the feedback, assistance and patience provided by Marianne and Kathryn throughout the writing, and the inevitable delays, were invaluable.

I'm grateful to all the tutors and lecturers at Brunel who provided their valuable time, thoughts and quotes. They are, in no particular order: Emily Danvers, head of the Academic Skills team; Dr Fiona Cullen, Youth & Community Work lecturer; Dr Martin Greenhow, lecturer in Maths; Dr Simon Kent, Computing lecturer (whose project management module also helped me a lot with another initiative I became involved in!); Alice MacKenzie, Occupational Therapy tutor; Dr Kelly Ashford, Sports Psychology tutor; Dr Mariann Rand-Weaver, Biosciences lecturer and tireless Pro-Vice Chancellor.

I received a lot of support from the staff I worked with in the Library – in particular, Ann and Lorna deserve a mention. Emily, who I'm proud to mention twice in the list, and Courtney, were wonderful colleagues who continue to make Brunel's Academic Skills service the envy of the sector! I must also mention Sarah Williams at Cardiff Metropolitan, who instilled in me my interest in helping students improve their writing.

My unexpected but never-regretted move – to work with online learning while writing this book – could have disrupted things considerably. Paal Elgvad, having taken me under his wing, made this transition as smooth as possible and has accepted last-minute pleas for days off with almost saintly virtue and good cheer!

My family, of course, provided incredible encouragement. My brothers, Laurence and Conrad, provided drive by reading sections, commenting, and lamenting that they didn't have a book like this when they were studying. Thanks to my mother Magda and my father Jonathan, who inspired me to work in academia, and who also provided some of the quotes used in this book. My friends – Sarah, Eimear and Ellie in particular – put up with my behaviour during the most stressful times, and celebrated with me during the better ones.

And, of course, Kate, who was far, far too patient with me – much more than I deserved. She was always there – and will continue, I hope, to be there – to say the right things at the right time.

Introduction

The Aims of this Book and How to Use It

Writing at university

Writing essays and assignments is difficult. I imagine most of my readers agree with that statement. Understanding what is expected of you at university level, and then meeting these high academic standards, are daunting skills. In fact, you'll never be finished: it is always possible to improve your essay-writing skills, and to make your written work more effective.

What is more, writing effective, high-quality assignments *should* be difficult. Being able to write essays on complex topics to a high standard is a skill worth having. Studying at university gives you the perfect opportunity to develop it. Of course, you must also develop these skills to get the marks needed to pass your course!

One of the things that makes this even *more* difficult (apart from the wide range of challenges that come with studying in higher education) is the fact that you are expected to develop these skills while you are studying for your degree: a whole, complex subject.

At university, you're expected to develop in-depth knowledge and analytical skills in fields like, for example, business, computing, creative writing or philosophy, and, *in addition*, the writing skills to express this knowledge effectively.

My experience working in higher education has taught me that most students are eager to spend time developing their writing skills – as well as other academic skills, such as effective presenting, statistics and time management.

Because these skills will be developed while you are studying an academic subject, you want to be sure that this time is spent *wisely*. This is true of *all* time spent on studying.

Take this situation, for example: if you went to see your personal tutor to discuss a part of her most recent lecture, you would want to make the most of the appointment time you had. You would hope to come away with some meaningful, practical advice.

'Meaningful, practical advice' is a phrase that neatly summarises what I hope this book provides. The book's focus is relatively narrow compared with other books about study skills. The spotlight is largely directed at the basic concepts behind the grammar of academic English, and the conventions of academic writing. More advanced chapters discuss specific techniques to make your writing effective.

By keeping this focus clear and strong throughout the book, I hope to: help you develop your essay writing; make it more effective; and make you aware of the common mistakes or issues that can often lead to lost marks (but, with a bit of work, don't have to).

When the book's focus does become slightly wider (the chapter on referencing, for example), the aim is still to provide to-the-point, practical advice that you can quickly apply to your own written work. The techniques discussed in chapters like this are still those that are vital for improving the quality of the sentences and paragraphs on the pages you write.

This book, then, sticks pretty closely to your writing itself – to the phrases, words and paragraphs on the page. You will find a range of books that tackle academic skills more generally. They might talk more about the planning process, about the structure of assignments, and, even further from the printed page, how to give presentations or manage your time.

Many of the books that discuss these things are excellent, but to keep my advice practical I have deliberately chosen a focus that I think matches many of the concerns students have while studying, especially early on in their studies.

I won't dwell on definitions for 'essay' and 'assignment', two words I use almost interchangeably. The rules of academic writing apply across all subjects, and although you will be asked to do different things in your assignments, similar things are expected of you. Any piece of written work longer than, say, 250 words is what this book calls an essay or assignment.

Another word I use throughout the book, and one I *do* want to define quickly, is 'argument'.

'Argument' in this sense doesn't mean a specific debate between two or more people around the kitchen table or at the pub! (That said, academia *is* all about debate; debate based on reason, however – not emotion).

That more common definition of argument actually comes from the classical idea – argument as a process of reasoning: that is, using evidence and logic to reach a conclusion. That sounds exactly like what should be happening in your essays, doesn't it?

In fact, the nature of writing, studying and learning at Western universities borrows much from classical Greek ideas. Using reason to convince your audience (in this case, your readers) of something (in this case, your answer or response to the essay question or assignment brief) is one of these concepts.

'Critical thinking' is another idea, a vital one while studying at university, which is descended from this classical tradition. Critical thinking is a frame of mind in which you analyse your research, don't take anything for granted and look at all sides of other arguments before reaching your own conclusion.

In Western Higher Education, this frame of mind, and this way of thinking, is the goal. This is opposed to simple memorisation of facts, and using essays to try and prove to the reader that you've done this memorisation. The book does not focus on critical thinking throughout, but there is a chapter that examines this topic, and how to use other sources in our work, in some detail.

In summary, when you read the word 'argument', I mean not just your essay as a whole, but your specific sequence of logical ideas, with their supporting evidence. This should all be written in a way that convinces your reader that your answer to the essay question is a valid, thoughtful one.

The basic idea behind learning in a British university, and what you are ultimately trying to do, is summarised neatly by Martin:

WHAT YOUR TUTORS SAY

'Seek to understand, rather than memorise facts' – Martin, Maths lecturer

---

In your essays, you are trying to demonstrate that you *understand* the key ideas underpinning your subject, not that you are particularly good at memorising dates, names or places. The chapter on critical thinking looks at specific techniques to help you demonstrate this, but it is a useful idea to have in the back of your mind as you read on.

Because you are trying to demonstrate a complex, high level of thinking, your writing should be *simple* and *clear* – another key theme this book will mention repeatedly!

What's in this book?

Below are summaries of each chapter. Seeing a brief explanation of the topics included in each chapter, and the order they're in, should help make the book's overall direction clear.

After this introduction, you'll read about:

Basic conventions of academic writing

There are certain rules you must follow in academic writing, and some conventions you have to stick to. There are reasons for this, which the chapter will make clear. Before getting stuck into complex grammatical issues, it will be useful to start with some of the rules you *need* to get your head around when writing essays.

Basic grammatical concepts

This chapter outlines some of the basic grammatical rules you should be comfortable with. The aim is not to learn hundreds of grammatical terms or memorise complex definitions. Instead, the focus is on understanding some fundamental rules, explained with examples from academic writing. You can then make sure to follow these rules, and to put the techniques to practical use in your work.

Putting sentences together

Basic grammar doesn't do much good unless you are actually writing whole sentences! This chapter builds on the previous two by looking at constructing effective, grammatically correct academic sentences – applying the rules and conventions you've already learned.

Putting paragraphs together

After discussing how sentences are put together, the next logical step is to look at how to arrange these sentences to make effective, well-written paragraphs. Some of the rules and ideas in this chapter are similar to those in the preceding one; however, there are also plenty of important additional techniques to bear in mind when writing paragraphs. They will be discussed here.

Critical thinking and referencing

Although this book's main focus is not on 'critical thinking' (a broad term that refers to a certain way of thinking about the sources or texts you're reading as part of your studies), referencing your research correctly is a vital part of academic writing. It is impossible to separate the mechanics of referencing from *how* we effectively bring our research into our own writing and our own arguments.

As such, this chapter is intended to provide a practical introduction to two things. The first is critical thinking; integrating what you read into your own work in an effective, thoughtful and honest way. The second is referencing, which is the *practical* or *technical* set of steps to show your reader exactly how and where you've used your sources.

Conciseness and clarity

The chapters up to this point have focused on aspects of academic writing that could be called *essential*. It is *essential* that you follow the academic conventions in Chapter 1; to get your sentences right it is *essential* that you apply the grammar rules from Chapter 2.

This chapter provides ideas, rather than rules, to help the development of your own writing and to make it effective *beyond* the essentials.

These key ideas, illustrated with examples, serve as a starting point. The techniques outlined in this chapter help make writing clear (effective and to-the-point) and concise (using only the necessary words to make an appropriate point). You'll learn that you have various techniques at your disposal. As you develop as a writer, you'll improve at using these techniques appropriately.

Common mistakes and how to deal with them

My experience giving students guidance on their written work has highlighted certain mistakes and issues that appear too commonly in assignments. These mistakes are made by students at all levels of study and ability. This chapter tackles the main ones, with examples and solutions for each.

I hope that you can dip in and out of this chapter and find something to double-check in your own work. Because I've based this chapter on my extensive experience of reading many different kinds of academic writing, I'm confident that it effectively deals with problems and issues that, in most cases, can be avoided quite easily.

Proofreading effectively

This chapter provides guidance on a vital, but often neglected, part of the writing process: proofreading your work. This chapter discusses techniques to help you ensure that your work is ready for submission, and ready for others to read.

Notes on the text and the conventions I follow

The final part of this chapter highlights a few things you need to be aware of as you read this book. It focuses on the conventions and techniques I use in the following chapters.

Different subjects

The examples of academic writing I use come from a range of different academic subjects. I wrote all of them myself, and as such you should not treat them as factual representations of any topic.

Similarly, all the references I use in the examples are made up. Your focus should be on *applying* the ideas that the examples demonstrate. Learn specific *techniques* from the examples and think about using them in your own work. Don't look for actual content in any of my examples.

Most of the actual ideas and themes discussed in this book, and the key points I make, apply to academic writing on any subject. Whether you are studying social care or sports psychology, computer science or creative writing, law or linguistics, physics or physiotherapy (I have taught academic writing sessions to all the subjects I've just named), the principles behind academic writing will be the same.

Referencing

In my example sentences and paragraphs, I use the Harvard referencing system. As you'll discover in the chapter 'Critical thinking and referencing', there are many different referencing styles or systems. More detail will be provided on some of them. There are also principles that apply to all referencing styles.

Put simply, Harvard referencing involves including the surnames of the authors of your source material in brackets. These brackets go inside sentences at appropriate points in your text, along with the year the source material was published.

For the sake of simplicity, I wanted to choose *one* style and stick with it. I use the Harvard style because it is relatively simple and used by many UK universities across a range of subjects. As mentioned above, all the references I use are *fictional* and I use them to demonstrate writing techniques only. In most cases the names of authors I use are fictional.

Key Point

It's important that you bear in mind that the writing in this book doesn't *strictly* follow all the conventions of academic writing that I tell you about. This book is not an essay. Additionally, is not an academic text in the same way most of your textbooks are.

To maintain a friendly and accessible tone, there are some techniques I use that you should avoid in your essays.

Because this is such an important fact, I will repeat it at appropriate points throughout the book.

To summarise, however, so you have an idea going forward:

I use the second person 'you' to address my readers throughout the book. As you'll learn in the next chapter, this is not acceptable in academic writing.

Similarly, I use the first person 'I' and 'my' to refer to myself. This is something to avoid in *most* essays. Some subjects involve a kind of writing called 'reflective' writing, in which the author of an essay discusses their own experiences in an academic context. Outside of this particular type of academic writing, however, the first person and references to yourself as the author of a piece of work should not appear.

You should not use 'contractions', in which words are joined together, and letters removed, to be replaced with an apostrophe. For example, 'won't' is the contracted form of 'will not'. I use some contractions to maintain this sense of friendliness that would not be appropriate in an academic essay.

Finally, I use some phrases that could be deemed colloquial; some that might even be considered slang.

Key Point

As you can see above, I use these 'Key point' boxes throughout the book. They emphasise certain key ideas or points, or highlight specific examples of a certain technique. Some chapters have several boxes like this, and some of them only have a few.

I don't have any specific rules for each box, and I hope everything I've written is important. However, if I think a certain point should stand out from the rest of the text it'll appear in a box like this.

WHAT YOUR TUTORS SAY

Throughout the book, you'll also see these 'What your tutors say' boxes. Experienced academics who teach a range of subjects (I give the subject with their name) have kindly provided me with their thoughts and tips on many of the things I write about in this book.

(Continued)

(Continued)

I only use first names in the text itself, but you can find more information about who they are in the Acknowledgements.

These brief quotations give you the chance to hear from the kinds of people who will actually be marking your work. In most cases, I use the quotes from the lecturers to begin a discussion of my own, or to reinforce a point I am making. This actually parallels the kind of thing you should aim to do when you reference other sources.

Now that I've introduced the topic, let's get on with it!

1

Basic Conventions of Academic Writing

My aim in this chapter is to highlight the main, basic conventions of academic writing. A 'convention' is, in some cases, a rule to follow, or it can be a technique your tutors expect to see used in your assignments. Your lecturers, professors and other tutors have to follow these same rules when they publish books and journal articles.

If you are used to writing essays, you may find that you are familiar with much of this material, some of which I would consider 'basic'. If you're just starting at university, or haven't studied for a while, some of these ideas might be newer to you.

Read this section carefully. It's surprising how often students submit essays with these conventions ignored or misused. 'How' to write at university is just as important as 'what' to write. The two go together.

WHAT YOUR TUTORS SAY

'Correct grammar and referencing, indicates that you care about how you present yourself.' – Mariann, Biosciences lecturer

---

Mariann makes this same point: your knowledge of a particular subject, and the content of your answer to an essay question, by themselves are not enough to satisfy the tutors marking your work. You are expected to engage with the academic debate in an academic way, and 'present yourself' accordingly.

Mariann mentions grammar and referencing; this also applies to academic conventions.

As you progress through your studies, this material will become more familiar. Most of these conventions apply to presentations too. Becoming comfortable with these basic rules is greatly helped by the *reading* we have to do as part of our time at university.

When you read a journal article for your next seminar, or learn how to perform a particular experiment from a textbook, or are simply picking relevant books from the library shelves, don't just focus on the *content*, as important as that is. Try and absorb the way these conventions come up again and again in all the academic writing you'll have to *read*.

It's really important to pay close attention to your reading, beyond its content. This is *the* best way of developing your own writing. Books like this, and the academic skills workshops your university runs, are important; but only if you are doing the reading expected of you, and then *more*. I have already mentioned this, and will continue to repeat this point throughout the book, because it is a vital, overlooked and very *simple* way of slowly developing and improving your own writing.

Why does academic writing have rules? Good academic writing has various qualities; it is clear, formal, objective and supported.

Additionally, because you are writing about potentially complex ideas, it should be as simple as possible, in order to make these ideas clear. So academic writing might end up being complex, but you should never *try* to write things in a complex way. Discuss your ideas at a high enough level, and the complexity is almost like the 'side effect' you get with medicines; it is not an actual objective of your writing. At university, you'll be discussing serious and important ideas a lot of the time, and complexity will naturally grow out of that.

More examples of some other academic techniques appear in the chapter, 'Common Mistakes and How to Deal With Them'. In that chapter I also provide more examples of how issues appear and how to resolve them. The aim of this chapter is to *introduce* you to the *basic* conventions. After that, we can look at grammatical issues and the process of actually putting an argument together. This list is not meant to be exhaustive, but I have tried to cover the most important and common conventions.

Before we go on to discuss some conventions one-by-one, it's worth noting one final point. This book does not stick to all of them. I intended to write a friendly, easygoing guide. You already have plenty of reading to do as part of your course. I've explained how important it is that you take the time to learn from that too!

Although my writing is *relatively* formal, the level of formality is occasionally lower than would be expected of your essays – the exclamation mark I used in the previous sentence, for example, and the way I address my readers as 'you', are examples of features in my writing that would not be appropriate in an academic essay. Where this point is particularly important, I'll highlight it again.

Using acronyms

Acronyms are words grouped together then referred to by their first letters. You're likely to encounter many in an academic environment. Here are some examples: BBC, HEI, USA, IT.

These must be written in a particular way in academic writing. This is an excellent example of a simple convention that, followed properly, makes writing clearer. In a 'normal' length essay (anything less than, say, 8000 words), simply write the term out *in full* and indicate the acronym in brackets afterwards. After this, you can just use the acronym. Here's an example:

> ✓ The budget cuts proposed raised doubts among officials at the Ministry of Defence (MoD). A spokesman for the MoD confirmed discussions were ongoing.

After the example sentence, the acronym 'MoD' could be used.

If you a writing a longer piece of work, like a dissertation, it might be worth occasionally 'reminding' your readers of a particular acronym. You might use the full phrase the first time you use it in each chapter. Another option, particularly if a piece of work contains many different acronyms, is to have a glossary or appendix that lists them all in one place. Ask your tutor what kind of techniques they would like you to use.

Key Point

There are some acronyms which don't need to be given in full. It is unlikely, for example, that you'll need to write 'United Kingdom' instead of UK, because this is common knowledge. I'd also say the same about 'USA'. If in doubt, however, write the full term first, as I did in the example. You will need to exercise judgement as to which acronyms won't need to be written in full – but *most* of them will.

Establishing objectivity

'Objectivity' is a quality you need your assignments to have. What does it mean to be objective when you write?

Objectivity refers to a deliberate distance between yourself as a writer and the subject matter of your assignment. Being objective is about creating this distance. Objectivity is established in various ways. I discuss some of these ways separately: for example, avoiding the first and second person (discussed later in the chapter) is a way of establishing objectivity by making your writing seem less 'familiar'.

Some students find it useful to think about the opposite of objectivity – 'subjectivity'. If you are writing in a *subjective* way, you seem very close to your subject. Another way to think about this difference is this: imagine objectivity as being on the outside looking in. Subjectivity is being on the inside looking out.

So, instead of writing about your own experiences, you write about the research and reading you've done. Instead of making points based on your *opinions*, write about the conclusion to which your research has led you. Instead of writing based on a chat, or argument, you had with your friends, use an interview you've conducted with an academic *expert* in the field.

There is an important exception to be aware of. Some subjects at university involve a kind of academic writing called 'reflective writing'. Reflective writing is about your reflections on experiences you've had; they will be experiences relevant to the topic, or to your course. Writing a report on a work placement you completed, for example, would involve reflection. Reflective assignments ask you to discuss what you've learned from certain experiences, in the context of the theory you've been taught and the academic texts you've read.

More examples include teaching-based courses: you might be asked to write about your week teaching at a school. If you are undertaking any kind of work placement on, for example, an engineering course, you might be assigned to write a diary or some kind of summary of what you did and what you learned. Similarly, if you complete a group project, writing up the way the group made decisions and worked together (which would clearly include you as a member of the group) might also involve recounting your own experiences.

This section has made clear the importance of being objective. Following and understanding some of the other conventions in this chapter will actually help you achieve objectivity in your academic writing.

Using colloquial language or contractions, for example, makes writing seem subjective. This is because your reader will get the impression that you are less serious (and not thinking in an academic way) about your subject.

The first and second person (words like 'I', 'you', etc.) use very *personal* nouns that decrease the distance between writer and subject. Use the third person to create that distance. *Reference* the work of other academics, researchers and authors to show your engagement with the academic debate on a topic.

Below I provide two examples from an essay about the principles community workers need to be aware of during their work. Each sentence is making a similar, though not identical point. One is obviously *subjective*, with little or no distance between the writer and the topic. By contrast, the second is *objective*, and so has established this distance.

Compare:

> ✗ I would feel really hurt if someone passed on personal information about me without my knowledge.

with

> ✓ Community workers must follow ethical conventions so as not to undermine trust.

Both make a valid point. The first sentence, however, makes the point in a very personal way. The use of the first person 'I' reinforces the sense that the writer is discussing a situation from *their own* frame of reference. The second sentence takes the key point, about ethical conventions, and makes it in a calm, objective way.

Referencing correctly

This book doesn't go into great detail about how to reference (the conventions of which will vary from course to course and university to university), but any guide to academic writing must mention it. This is a brief summary; I go into more detail about referencing in a later chapter.

WHAT YOUR TUTORS SAY

'It is essential that your work provides linkages and examples from appropriate academic sources to evidence and provide scholarly context to your work.' – Fiona, Youth & Community Work lecturer

---

Fiona uses the word 'essential': you will almost always be expected to reference other sources in your work. If you write an essay with no references, you will get very low marks. Think about the journals and books you've been reading on your course. They're likely to be full of references.

There are various other words and techniques associated with referencing. Various referencing styles and systems exist (you might hear about 'citing', 'footnotes', the 'Harvard style', 'numeric referencing', and much more). However, *referencing* as a whole means making it clear when the ideas, concepts, quotations, diagrams, definitions, images or arguments in your work come from elsewhere. 'Elsewhere' might mean other books, conferences, journal articles, online sources, and so on.

This will be discussed later on, but a *crucial* part of writing essays and assignments is engaging with the body of research, writing and discussion on a particular topic or subject. There will be a wide selection of ideas at a subject level, and additional debate and discussion about specific parts of the subject or topics within it.

There will always be debate and discussion on a subject. Studying at university level is a way of entering that debate. This is why you'll be made to read books, research, conduct laboratory experiments, and so on.

Referencing, however you are expected to do it, is how you'll point out that a particular quote, for example, came from a specific page in a specific book; or that a particular painting is very important to the history of art.

In short, almost every essay or assignment you write at university should contain references. Be aware that not every essay question you are assigned will explicitly say 'reference other sources in your answer' (some might do, if there are specific texts that you have to include, for example). This does not mean you won't be expected to engage with your reading material and prove that you have done so in your essay. This is expected of students to such an extent that sometimes it is not even pointed out.

In the chapter on critical thinking and referencing, and the final chapter about common mistakes, referencing *effectively* will be examined more closely. Different referencing styles are outlined: you'll need to double-check which one your tutors want you to use.

It will take a long time before you can remember exactly how to reference a particular source, especially an obscure one. Even your lecturers will sometimes have to look up an example for their own work. Whether or not you can do it from memory, you *will* have to reference properly and consistently.

Avoiding slang/colloquial language

Academic writing is formal. This is commonly accepted by most students. What sometimes is not grasped properly is *why* it is formal. Formality in academic writing doesn't come from deliberately writing difficult, complex sentences, or using complex words where simple ones would serve the same purpose. It comes from making sure that no inappropriate informal language, like slang, is used. This also reinforces the sense of objectivity.

If a writer uses familiar turns of phrase from their everyday colloquial language, the sense of distance from the content might be lost. An assignment written in this way would seem more like an informal, spoken 'chat' about a subject rather than an academic discussion.

Additionally, in most cases, academic writing should be *literal*. This means that words and phrases used should operate according to their actual dictionary definitions. Quite often, slang, and colloquial phrases from speech, are not literal. Here is an example of a common phrase that is not literal and, as such, would be inappropriate in an essay:

> ✗ It is widely accepted that election campaigns go the extra mile in their final weeks.

The phrase 'go the extra mile' means, in informal English, to make additional effort, to try harder. Taken literally, however, this sentence suggests that staff working on political campaigns travel an additional mile nearer election time! A simple, literal version of the sentence might look like this:

> ✓ It is widely accepted that election campaigns increase their efforts in the final weeks.

So what is slang? What is 'colloquial language'; what are 'colloquialisms'? You have just seen an example.

Although most students are aware that they should not use 'informal' language in essays, it is the definition of 'informal' or 'slang' that is more difficult. Unfortunately, this book can only help to a certain extent, and provide some guidelines.

In the following box are some examples, from essays on various subjects, of sentences that contain one or more colloquial words or phrases. Some of them are obviously informal, and might even make you laugh; others might surprise you. I will provide improved versions afterwards.

> ✗ Saddam Hussein was a bad dude.
> ✗ The company, in an attempt to cut costs, fired 5% of the workforce in 2004.
> ✗ Most of the research cited here concludes with the question how come only two hearings in Parliament have been held about this issue.
>
> *(Continued)*

(Continued)

✗ Analysing the tendency of pop music to borrow from dance-based genres from a postmodern standpoint limits conclusions. The scene has never really focused on that kind of stuff.

✗ Bradshaw (2009) decides that the conclusion is clear as crystal: sporting activity should be promoted more to kids at a young age.

In the first sentence, 'bad dude' is almost laughably informal. 'Dude' is outright slang, and the word 'bad' is just as informal; even worse, 'bad dude' is a subjective value judgement that does not make a point in an academic way. A better idea would be to give the reader actual evidence as to why the author deems Saddam to have been a 'bad dude':

✓ Saddam Hussein, after coming to power, embarked on a totalitarian rule of systematic terror; a rule catalogued by many, over the years (Makiya, 1989; Johnson, 2005; Hitchens, 2007).

The second sentence would be acceptable in an essay, except for one word: the verb 'fired', which is actually a slang term. As you've learned, academic writing should be *literal*. Clearly, terminating employment has nothing to do with fire, or flames! Here, then, is an example of a word common in speech, but not suitable for an academic essay. This can be easily corrected by replacing the word:

✓ The company, in an attempt to cut costs, terminated the contracts of 5% of the workforce in 2004.

In the third sentence, the informal phrase – one that comes directly from spoken English – is perhaps harder to spot. It is the forming of a question with the words 'how come'. Going back to our idea of literal English, we can see that the phrase 'how come' does not really mean anything.

Think about what the question is really asking. How would someone actually ask the question? 'Why have only two hearings been held?', most likely. I can use this to replace the phrase 'how come':

> ✓ Most of the research cited here concludes by questioning why only two hearings in Parliament have been held about this issue.

The fourth example contains two colloquial words or phrases, both in the second sentence.

First, the word 'stuff' is inappropriate in academic writing. It is not literal, and is also vague and informal – three things you do not want your writing to be described as! The phrase 'kind of stuff' is even vaguer, and makes the problem worse.

It is common to describe a particular fanbase as a 'scene' in speech, but here it should be replaced. Imagine this sentence being read by someone for whom English was not a first language. Slang phrases like this will not have the same meaning for them; another reason we should be literal in our words and phrases.

As you'll learn later in the book, the word 'really' rarely adds anything to academic writing (the same goes for 'very'). It doesn't mean much or give the reader any real information. As such, it adds to the informality of the sentence, and should be removed.

Here, then, is a possible adapted version of the second sentence:

> ✓ Analysing the tendency of pop music to borrow from dance-based genres from a postmodern standpoint limits conclusions. The contemporary fanbase of popular music tends not to focus on concepts like these.

The final problem sentence contains one 'cliché', as well as an instance of informal language. In addition, there is another problem with it. It is a different kind of problem, one that this book discusses later, but I will point it out anyway.

The phrase 'clear as crystal' is a 'cliché'. Clichés are common or stock phrases unique to a particular language, and overused in that language. Most clichés, a long time ago, were interesting ways of describing something, and have been used so often so as to become popular, and to lose their original effect.

Most people know them, and they are frequently used in speech. Every language has its own clichéd phrases, almost all of them too informal for academic writing.

Many clichés in the English language are based around describing things in subjective ways, which you should avoid in academic writing. Other examples include 'a diamond in the rough'; 'frightened to death'; 'read between the lines'. You'd never have cause to use many of them in an essay, but there are a few that appear occasionally!

'Clear as crystal' can be replaced with one word; the most obvious and simple choice is shown below.

Another problem expression is 'kids'. Literal English is clear on this: 'kids' are juvenile goats (as people who disapprove of the word 'kids' often point out!). The word should be replaced with the most obvious alternative: children.

The last problem, of a different nature, is the final phrase in the sentence: 'at a young age'.

The word 'children', which replaces 'kids', has a definition: it means people at a young age; thus the phrase 'at a young age' is not needed. All it is doing is repeating an idea established by another word.

If the source writer mentions a *specific* age, or refers to children at primary school (or another specific group), then this should be made clear.

This allows two possible approaches:

✓ Bradshaw (2009) decides that the conclusion is clear: sporting activity should be promoted more to children.

✓ Bradshaw (2009) decides that the conclusion is clear: sporting activity should be promoted more to children at primary school age.

Everyone has some awareness of slang, and colloquial, informal language that they might use in speech. As the examples have shown, however, such language can be harder to detect than you might think.

In the examples, I deliberately ensured that, apart from the problematic phrases, the sentences were academically appropriate. It is quite easy to find, and to avoid writing, entirely colloquial sentences or paragraphs. The occasional informal phrase is more of a danger.

As you read through your work, ask yourself:

- Does each word or phrase mean what a dictionary says it means?
- Is this phrase commonly heard in speech?
- Would I expect to see this in the textbooks and journals I read as part of my course?
- Would someone not as familiar with English as I am translate this correctly?

Think about that last point: someone using an English dictionary to translate 'clear as crystal', from the last example we changed, would probably wonder why your essay was suddenly referring to jewels!

If any of your answers to these questions leaves you in doubt, take the approach we have just used. Replace the phrases you have concerns about with clear, effective, simple alternatives.

Avoiding emotive language

Avoiding emotive language is a skill similar to avoiding colloquial language. It is hard to define at first, but the more you write, the easier it will become.

Emotive language is not just language that could be described as 'emotional'. More than that, emotive language is used *deliberately* to evoke an emotion in the reader. This is common in some journalism, politics and fiction.

WHAT YOUR TUTORS SAY

'Rather than just arguing that, in your personal and/or professional opinion, young people are demonised by the media, provide examples, and cite scholarly work that further supports your observation. Such an approach will prevent tutors writing "evidence?" repeatedly in the margins of your assignments.' – Fiona, Youth & Community Work lecturer

---

Fiona uses a specific example of a potentially emotive topic from her own area of expertise – the 'demonisation' of young people. She recommends using effective referencing from other sources to make it clear you are not just writing, in a subjective way, about your opinions. As you'll see, this is good advice about a very effective technique.

Academic writing involves making points based on evidence. Clearly, then, you do not want to use emotive language in assignments. You must avoid deliberately appealing to the emotions of your readers. Because you might be writing about a subject that has the potential to affect emotions, or provoke a powerful reaction, this can be difficult.

What *is* emotive language, though? Some words and phrases can be emotive in themselves. Others might be perfectly acceptable in an essay unless used as part of a particular phrase or in an emotive way. This is one of the conventions that you have to think carefully about.

Ultimately, you must use your common sense. Emotive language tends to be subjective, like colloquial language. The more you develop an objective writing style, the more naturally you will avoid emotive language.

Unfortunately, it is impossible to put every word in the dictionary into either a column titled 'emotive' or a column titled 'not emotive'! There are some words and phrases in the box below. I'd argue that they could probably be considered emotive regardless of the context in which they're used. You should get an idea from this list of the kind of language associated with *emotional* rather than *logical* arguments.

- ✗ Horrible

- ✗ Disgraceful

- ✗ Disgusting

- ✗ Incredible

- ✗ Magnificent

- ✗ Dire

- ✗ Tragedy

- ✗ Wonderful

- ✗ Inflict

Key Point

The word 'tragedy', included in the above list, is commonly used in an emotive way in some journalism. However, it would be perfectly appropriate to use the term to refer to a play from the tragic genre (like many of Shakespeare's works). Understanding the vocabulary associated with your subject will help you differentiate between the appropriate and emotive use of certain words or phrases.

Here are some short example sentences, from a range of academic subjects, that could reasonably be described as emotive.

- ✗ Many studies (Hurford, 1982; Ryan, 1990; Jackson & Devon, 2002) reinforce the idea that environmental deregulation in Western states can leave parts of otherwise modern, thriving countries as treacherous, barren wasteland.

- ✗ The creation of the NHS by the wartime government of Britain was a towering, even dizzying, achievement.

- ✗ In the play, after the character's baby is born, the torment and turmoil that the family endures is sickening.

> ✗ Where policies like this have been implemented in secondary schools, the schools have raced up league tables.
>
> ✗ Recent coverage of women's sport in the UK has, sadly, paid almost no attention whatsoever to athletic ability, instead, focusing – in a puerile way – on the appearance of the sportswomen.

Two points are worth noting immediately: emotive language is not only associated with *negative* portrayal of a topic. Language can be used to evoke positive emotions; either way, it is not appropriate in academic writing.

Emily, below, points out a problem with any subjective language – her example word is a positive one.

WHAT YOUR TUTORS SAY

'Be wary of using emotive language in your work. Even a word like "good" is problematic as it is subjective and can't be tested or measured. Good according to whom?' – Emily, Academic Skills lecturer

---

Second, many of these sentences might be making valid points. The first one, for example, references several studies. Just because a sentence contains emotive language does not mean it is 'wrong' – the point just has to be made in an objective way. See Emily's question: 'good according to whom'?

As you can see, most (though not all) emotive language appears as description. Descriptive words (adjectives and adverbs) are discussed in the next chapter – you'll learn that they don't contribute much to academic writing. In the case of emotive description, they can damage your writing. By avoiding descriptive language and only using it when absolutely necessary, you are reducing the risk of using emotive language.

In one example, however, the verb (action word – see the next chapter) is emotive. This is the verb 'raced' in the fourth example. The author is trying to use a *descriptive* verb that does not just describe an action, but gives a sense of *how* the action occurs. However, in this case, it is exaggerated to the point that it becomes an emotive sentence.

Avoiding exaggeration, and exaggerated description in particular, is the best tactic to avoid emotive language – and this is likely to reduce your use of colloquial language too.

Because these sentences are making points to provoke a strong reaction in the reader, simply rephrasing them is not sufficient. You, as the author, have to decide on the evidence you can use to highlight the conclusion you are going to make. This is why I am not going to provide improved examples of all of the above sentences; so much depends on context.

I will improve one of them, however, to demonstrate the process. Here is the original, analysing the relationship between gender and sport:

> ✗ Recent coverage of women's sport in the UK has, sadly, paid almost no attention whatsoever to athletic ability, instead, focusing – in a puerile way – on the appearance of the sportswomen.

First, I'll identify the emotive language in the sentence: the word 'sadly', which might be acceptable if the rest of the sentence did not take such an emotive approach; the word 'whatsoever', which makes the claim seem more exaggerated; and the word 'puerile', which is not supported by any evidence, and seems to be the author's view.

To improve this sentence, I'd recommend the following steps: incorporate evidence into the sentence; find examples of the reactions of others to the coverage being discussed – this will make the writing seem less subjective; remove description that cannot be supported by evidence; and make it clear *why* a situation is 'sad' and must be improved, using a combination of evidence and the author's own conclusions.

The result might be something like this:

> ✓ Recent coverage of women's sport in the UK has, a variety of research concludes (Darking, 2009; Christopher & Wilson, 2010; Henderson, 2011), not focused enough on the sporting ability of sportswomen. This has generated some fierce reaction; Henderson references an interview in which a female footballer accused commentary of being 'puerile' (p24). The research points to the seriousness of the situation, which, regrettably, impacts negatively on gender relationships in younger people (Howard, 2010); a different approach is needed to change this situation.

The second version still expresses the idea that the situation is bad, and even demonstrates the emotional reactions that some people have shown – without being emotional or emotive itself. The references prove that there is agreement that the situation should change, and that there are far-reaching consequences that will continue if it does not.

Ultimately, emotive language, like colloquial language, tends to be subjective, descriptive and exaggerated. The more you base your ideas in evidence, and demonstrate that you are doing so, the more effective your work will be. If there are powerful emotions involved in a debate, demonstrate this by providing examples of them: but do not display your own, or deliberately try to provoke them in your readers.

Avoiding the first person

The 'first person' is a grammatical term for using the words 'I', 'we', 'us', 'ours', 'my', and so on. In the next section on basic grammar, you'll learn more about different types of words. The examples I've just provided, to show you what the first person consists of, are *pronouns*. They can be singular ('I' and 'me' – just referring to you as a single person) or plural ('ours' and 'us' – you are part of a group, perhaps).

The first person is common in many kinds of writing (especially fiction) and in speech. Academic writing is very different – its aim is not to entertain or inform in a popular way, but to make an argument that engages with the academic discussion on a subject.

In this book, I use both the first person and the second person, which I discuss below. Although my writing here is fairly formal, use of the first person was a *deliberate* decision on my part to make the text seem 'friendlier' (and, indeed, less objective).

Students often ask 'Can I use the first person in my essays?'. Unfortunately, the answer is more complex than just 'no', but not much more complex. If in doubt, do *not* use the first person. Avoid it completely. Sometimes your tutors, or your course handbook, will explicitly tell you not to write in the first person; this makes things easier for you!

Sometimes, however, you might come across use of the first person in your reading, and sometimes you might need to use it in your writing. Very experienced academic writers sometimes use the first person in various ways. The aim here, however, is to become comfortable with the *basic* conventions of academic writing. As such, we will ignore some of these ways in which the first person can be used for effect, and look at the *main* exception to the rule 'do not use the first person in academic writing'.

The main exception is the 'reflective' writing I have already mentioned.

Reflective writing involves reflection on things that have happened to *you*. You cannot pretend they happened to someone else, so you write about them in the first person. It will usually be clear if your assignment requires this kind of reflection. If you are in doubt, ask your tutor if he or she expects use of the first person (which is usually unavoidable in reflective writing).

Avoiding the second person

The *second* person is, as you might have guessed, a way of directly addressing someone else. Second person pronouns include 'you', 'your' and 'yours'. Some languages have a different word for the plural 'you' (several people being addressed directly) and the singular 'you' (just one person), but English does not.

However, the second person in English has a very distinct purpose beyond allowing you to talk or write to people (imagine writing a text or email to a friend without using 'you'!). It is used, quite often, in a *general* way, meaning 'people'. This is very common in spoken English.

I'll give you some examples to show you what I mean:

> ✗ If you want a career in engineering, you will have to show dedication and focus.

Now, if this is a careers advisor speaking to a specific student or group of students, then the second person is entirely appropriate (though it wouldn't be an example of academic writing). However, if you write this in an essay about the engineering industry, you are talking *generally*. Substitute 'people' for 'you' and the sentence means the same thing. Substitute, then, 'people' for the first 'you', and the pronoun 'they' for the second 'you'. Using 'you' twice would result in an odd sentence. This leaves you with:

> ✓ If people want a career in engineering, they will have to show dedication and focus.

Here's an example from an English essay, discussing poetry:

> ✗ You really have to read Donne's poetry aloud to fully appreciate his use of language.

Again, what the student here means by 'you' is 'the reader'. While *you*, reading the essay, might technically be called the reader, it is reasonable to assume the student is not addressing *you*, because he or she is addressing *everyone* reading the assignment.

Unlike the use of the first person, the second person should simply be *completely avoided in all academic writing*. When students use the second person in an essay (this is, unfortunately, a *very* common issue) it is almost always in the general way. This makes writing very informal because it is an aspect of spoken English. Remember, to create objectivity and a sense of academic discussion, things we might *say* as part of a less formal conversation might not be appropriate in academic writing.

It is very easy to check if you have used the second person in a typed assignment. Almost all word processors have a 'find' tool – use it, and search for the word 'you'. It will highlight the word wherever it appears. It will also find 'your' because the first three letters are the same.

Then, simply ask yourself, '*who* do I actually mean?' and make this clear. If you are using it in the general way (which is likely), rephrase the sentence. Work out what key point you are making and write clearly and simply in the third person.

Take the example from the English essay, above. The sentence is making a basic, and potentially valid, point – that Donne's work is better appreciated, or understood, read aloud. The sentence can be rewritten in several ways to say that quite clearly, with no use of the second person 'you'. One way of doing this might be:

✓ Donne's work is best appreciated when spoken aloud.

An alternative sentence would be:

✓ Reading Donne's work aloud gives the reader a better sense of the poems.

Both are simple and clear and make the same point without using the second person. The important thing here is not to think too hard about how to remove the 'you'; just do it as *simply as you can*.

Here is another example:

✗ The financial crisis in 2008 showed that sometimes you can't rely on the opinions of experts because nobody predicted the crisis.

'You' is being used in the general way. The basic point of the sentence can easily be expressed without 'you'; here is just one possibility:

> ✓ Most experts failed to predict the financial crisis in 2008, which highlights the problem of relying on expert opinion.

There is another important rule to remember when resolving this problem. Students, finding they've used the second person 'you', sometimes think it's appropriate to replace it with the first person 'we' instead.

This is not common in speech, but for some reason is intended to serve a similar purpose to 'you' in essays. I'm not sure why students do this, but I have read it so many times I wanted to warn you here *not* to simply replace the second person 'you' with 'we'. For example:

Do *not* change

> ✗ You can't understand the conflict between Russia and Georgia in 2008 without an awareness of the region's history.

to

> ✗ We can't understand the conflict between Russia and Georgia in 2008 without an awareness of the region's history.

but instead to something like:

> ✓ An awareness of the region's history is needed to understand the conflict between Russia and Georgia in 2008.

In short: do not use the second person, and when removing it, do not simply replace it with the first person. Use the more objective third person instead.

Avoiding contractions

A 'contraction' is one word, made up of two or more words that have been joined together. Some letters from the words are left out and replaced with an apostrophe.

The apostrophe is a piece of punctuation that is misused in many ways. Some of these are discussed in the chapter on basic grammar, and in the chapter on common mistakes. Here, I focus exclusively on contractions – specifically, *not* using them in academic writing. This is another convention I have *not* rigidly followed in this book.

Examples are not hard to find, particularly in speech, or popular writing:

- 'Cannot' in its contracted form is 'can't'
- 'Will not' becomes 'won't'
- 'He is' or 'he has' become 'he's'
- 'Should not' becomes 'shouldn't'
- 'There will' becomes 'there'll'

The rule is simple: do not use contractions in academic writing.

Luckily, as with some of the other conventions, contractions are quite easy to find during your proofreading process. Just type an apostrophe into the 'find' tool of your word processor and you can examine the apostrophes you have used, one-by-one.

This will, of course, mean checking apostrophes used for other reasons (like possessives, or when quoting other sources; both will be mentioned later in the book). However, as soon as you see an apostrophe used in a contraction, you can just type the words out in full. It is certainly not worth losing marks because of an issue so easily fixed.

Simplicity, clarity and conciseness

This is not a single convention, but a broader issue of writing style. The example discussed below is longer than the previous examples in this chapter, and it involves more complex issues.

The later chapter called, unsurprisingly, 'Conciseness and Clarity', looks in more detail at specific techniques to make your writing effective. However, the sooner you start thinking about this issue, the better you will be at putting it into practice.

The three ideas are so intertwined I will not separate them. Essentially, you should use as few words as possible to make a point (conciseness); these *individual* words should be as straightforward as they can be without being informal or inappropriate (simplicity); and they should be put together in a way that makes your point effective and easy-to-understand (clarity).

This is a key theme of the book in a way that the other subsections of this chapter are not (this book is not, for example, all about acronyms). Writing simply, concisely and clearly is, however, a key *convention* of academic writing.

In fact, it is a key theme of the book *because* it is an essential convention of academic writing.

For now, I'm going to take one example and discuss it in some detail. In the same way that many of these conventions reinforce objectivity in writing, many also reinforce *clarity*. Conciseness is a feature of our writing that we have to learn to perfect ourselves. It is difficult!

Take a look at the two extracts below. Then you can read my explanation of the changes.

> ✗ To succeed in obtaining and achieving the highest possible marks in assignments, students must engage in a genuine and concerted attempt to conduct extensive research, devote much time to the planning process, and finally ensure they are entirely comfortable and confident with the rules of English grammar.

> ✓ To receive the highest possible marks in assignments, students must research effectively, spend enough time planning, and make sure they are confident with grammar.

Would you agree that the two extracts say very similar things? I'd argue that they say practically identical things. The first is over-the-top, unnecessarily formal and repetitive, and overlong. We do not need to labour our points. The second is clearly much shorter, which will give you valuable space to make more points, or support this one with references.

What follows is an outline of my thought process and reasoning behind the changes I've made; as you can see, I've rephrased/reworded large parts of the first version, as well as deleting sections. Everyone will do this kind of thing differently, and there are many different ways I could have altered the first example. So rather than seeing my explanation as a 'solution' to a specific problem, try and see it as an example of one approach to the convention of writing clearly and concisely. Try and view it, also, as showing you the kind of state of mind you should be in when you edit what you've written.

This following section is quite detailed. You might need to return to this part of the book. For now, read over this a few times – you'll see how many techniques and approaches to writing there are, and how many choices you have to make. The more you read, and the more you write and adopt these conventions, the more naturally you will think about the following kinds of points.

With all that in mind, let's take a look at why I changed the extract:

To begin with, the sentence is too long. Even if I hadn't managed to shorten it as much as I have, I would have broken it down into several shorter sentences.

Read it aloud and you will probably end up breathless. This is a sure sign a sentence is too long. Sentences that make you breathless are also likely to be too complex.

I thought that 'To succeed in obtaining and achieving the highest possible marks' could be reduced to 'to get the highest possible marks'. Surely using the verbs 'obtaining' *and* 'achieving' is unnecessary. These two words are doing the same thing in the sentence. The student is doing the same thing with the marks – receiving them.

I *could* have used the verb 'to get', but 'get' can often seem informal. 'Get' can be a troublesome verb. Many languages that are similar to English do not have a direct equivalent.

Key Point

Here is another quick example that illustrates potential problems with the word 'get'. Compare 'the patient got better' and 'the patient recovered'. The second is more formal, and shorter too.

Moving on, I've shortened 'students must engage in a genuine and concerted attempt to conduct extensive research'. In the second sentence I replace this with 'students must research effectively'.

Ask yourself: if you go into the library, eager to write your best essay yet, and you 'engage in a genuine and concerted attempt to conduct extensive research', what are you actually doing? You are researching *well*. That wasn't formal enough, so I went with *effectively*, which means a similar thing. You are researching in a way that provides you with lots of great points to go into your essay. I could also have used 'thoroughly'.

Key Point

The other difference here, which this book discusses further later on, is that I have used a stronger verb. 'Research', a key academic concept, is used as a verb, an action word – 'to research'. In the original, 'research' was a noun. There were two verbs – 'engage' and 'conduct'. Neither mean anything without the nouns 'attempt' and 'research' attached to them.

It is better to use effective, strong verbs. Again, think of the difference between 'I conduct research into endangered animals' and 'I research endangered animals'. The verb in the second sentence is stronger, carries more meaning on its own, and because of this the sentence is shorter without losing any of its message.

My updated version of the first extract is certainly not the best or only reworking possible. I could have written, 'students must research extensively and effectively', but I decided that if you are researching effectively, your research is probably extensive too.

My second version has, perhaps, lost the sense of a student trying hard. This can be seen in the first version in the phrase 'a genuine and concerted attempt'. To emphasise that idea of *trying* as well as 'effectiveness', I might write the sentence differently. An example might be: 'students must make the effort to research effectively'.

Next, I changed 'devote much time to the planning process' to 'spend enough time planning'. I thought 'devote' sounded a bit over-the-top, while 'spending' time is perfectly fine. That said, I have, as above, perhaps lost the sense of intense effort.

My worry, though, was that the first extract was not only unnecessarily formal, but seemed too hyperbolic. 'Hyperbole' means deliberately writing or speaking with exaggeration to have a specific effect. This is a technique commonly used in political speeches or opinion-writing. Academic writing should make arguments reinforced by evidence, research and reason.

You'll notice that I also removed the word 'much' from 'much time planning'. The phrases 'a lot of' or 'lots of' are often too vague and informal for academic writing. So you might find yourself writing 'much' or 'many' most of the time instead.

Here though, the word 'enough' is better, because it is more specific. Spending 'much' time is great, but how much is 'much'? A student needs to do the *right* amount of planning. That is, *enough* planning to form the structure of their work. Using 'enough' makes the meaning of the phrase clearer.

Is 'the planning process' all that different from just 'planning'? I'd argue that there is no difference. The 'planning' put into an assignment will include some specific processes. Because of this I used the simpler 'planning' and not 'the planning process'.

I also managed to considerably shorten the last phrase – 'finally ensure they are entirely comfortable and confident with the rules of English grammar'.

I removed the word 'finally' because the reader has come to the last point in the sentence – they *know* it is the 'final' point. My reader will see that a new paragraph begins after this sentence. They will understand from this that the subject is changing, or that I am making a different point. For these reasons I do not think it is necessary to label this 'finally'.

I replaced the verb 'ensure' with 'make sure'. I did not *have* to do this. Making this change has actually turned one word into two; as such, it has not made my work more concise. However, 'ensure' sounded a little too forced and formal to me. I don't think it makes a huge difference, but this is the approach I chose to take. Readers might disagree with me, and the sentence certainly makes sense without this change being made.

This in particular demonstrates quite effectively how writing is about making *choices* as an author. There are certain conventions to follow, but you will always have ultimate control over what goes onto the page.

I made a change to the last part of the sentence. I replaced 'entirely comfortable and confident with the rules of English grammar' with 'confident with grammar'. I removed 'entirely comfortable and confident' simply because I don't think this is true. Not many people ever become 'entirely' confident with English grammar, whether they are studying at university or not.

In fact, a key aim of this book is to help you develop an understanding of the *main* and most important aspects of grammar; the ones you need to write a decent essay or assignment. A fully comprehensive awareness of grammar is not necessary to do this.

Using both 'comfortable' *and* 'confident' is not necessary. It is likely that someone comfortable with a set of rules is confident with them too. There is no benefit, I'd argue, in using both words. I preferred confident, so left that in the sentence.

I removed the word 'English' from 'English grammar'. By getting rid of the reference to a specific language, I made the sentence more versatile. Its key point is broader and more accessible. Surely a writer should be confident with the grammar of whatever language they are working in?

This might seem like a great deal of work to go through to change a short paragraph. In reality, editing the paragraph won't take long – especially as you get used to thinking like this. You'll realise just how quickly you can make meaningful, effective adjustments to your work. One of the aims of this book is to help you develop your skills in this area.

Further reading

Copus, J (2009) *Brilliant Writing Tips for Students*. Basingstoke: Palgrave.

2

Basic Grammatical Concepts

This chapter focuses on some key grammatical concepts. These are the grammatical terms and ideas that are most important to ensure your writing is correct and effective.

Because the aim here is to provide practical advice, there is less detail than you might find in books that discuss English grammar as a topic in itself. Similarly, some grammar books are designed to help people learning English as a foreign language. These go into more detail about complex grammatical concepts. At the end of this chapter, you'll find some books that focus on English grammar more specifically, with exercises and tests to complete.

In this chapter, however, the aim is not for you to learn the names of every type of word there is. Nor do you need to memorise or understand some of grammar's more complex ideas.

Having a basic understanding of the key ideas in this chapter should suffice for now. As well as a definition for each key idea, there is a section on effective use. Reading these sections and applying them to your work should ensure that this chapter has a direct impact on your writing.

The next chapter then moves beyond individual word types to examine how sentences are put together in effective, grammatically correct ways.

Before looking at the individual grammatical terms, take some encouragement from this advice:

WHAT YOUR TUTORS SAY

'To improve your writing, you need to write a lot.' – Simon, Computing lecturer

---

Grammar, sometimes just by reputation, can seem like a difficult, daunting subject. Remembering what Simon points out here can help you feel more positive about this!

Whether or not you memorise grammatical terms, or decide to research further into different types of nouns and verbs, the grammar in your writing will improve *the more you write*. This doesn't just apply to your grammar, of course; all aspects of your writing improve as writing becomes more natural to you.

Your writing will only improve if you *keep* writing, so as you begin studying this tricky subject, try and view each assignment as an opportunity to practise. Even better, the feedback from your tutors for each 'practice' will help you develop even more as a writer.

Types of words

Nouns, proper nouns, concrete nouns, abstract nouns and plurals

Nouns are naming words. They provide names or labels for 'things'. (You'll learn that verbs, on the other hand, are actions.) Every sentence in an essay will have one or more nouns in it (unless they are replaced by pronouns).

'Concrete' nouns are tangible, real things – things you could touch, see or be part of. The clue is in the word 'concrete'.

Examples of concrete nouns you might find in academic writing include:

Essay

Meeting (this can also be a verb, but here I mean a collection of people in a room – 'a meeting' or 'the meeting')

Experiment

Therapist

Equation

Library

'Abstract' nouns are nouns that do not refer to tangible things. Abstract nouns are still names, but you cannot touch or see an abstract noun. Abstract nouns are very common in academic writing, which often directly focuses on abstract concepts and ideas. Here are some examples:

Conclusion

Intelligence

Fear

Extravagance

Method

Proper nouns are the names for unique things: specific people, places, brands, companies, and so on. In English, 'proper' nouns begin with a capital letter. Otherwise, they function in sentences as other nouns do. Academic writing involves debate and discussion around existing research; as such, names of authors, experts, researchers and committees, as well as the names of the texts they've written, tend to be mentioned frequently. These are all proper nouns.

The opposite of a proper noun (so, the name for most nouns) is a 'common' noun.

Similarly, though it will vary by subject, the names of places, specific events, brands, companies and organisations will often appear. Take a moment to think about the kinds of proper nouns likely to come up in your subject.

Sometimes historical events or academic theories can become proper nouns. As you read in preparation for your assignments, look for the examples from your subject where this has happened. Proper nouns work the same way as other nouns do in sentences; the capital letter is the difference. Here are some examples:

Dr Hofmann

Karl Marx

Toyota

World War II

London

Mount Everest

Key Point

Most proper nouns are easy to identify. In academic writing, however, there are often certain nouns associated with certain subjects that have become proper nouns – I've mentioned this above. The best sources of information around this are the things you read as part of your studying. You will get used to using 'Marxism' as a proper noun, and history students will discover many more historical events beyond 'World War II' that are treated as proper nouns.

There are even examples of words that mean one thing when they take a capital letter, and a different thing when they are a normal noun. For example, 'Fascism', as a proper noun, refers specifically to the Italian political movement from the 1930s, as practised by the Italian Fascist Party under Mussolini; while 'fascism', the regular noun, refers to the broader set of far-right political ideologies. Ask your tutors if you are ever in doubt.

WHAT YOUR TUTORS SAY

'Don't overuse capital letters: "the king, the government, and the parliament"; *but*, "the reign of King Henry VIII, the National Government of 1931, and the Long Parliament".' – Jonathan, History lecturer

Sticking with history, Jonathan provides some specific examples of regular nouns that do not need capital letters that sometimes become proper nouns because they describe a unique, particular thing. It is very tempting to use capital letters for nouns that are simply associated with or used often in the subject we are studying.

As you research, look at where capital letters are used by other academics. Only use them when you have to.

Nouns that refer to multiple things are 'plurals'. In most cases, English nouns become plurals when either 's' or 'es' is added to the end of the word: for example, one 'deadline' is a singular noun; unfortunately, you might need to learn to manage your work when you have multiple 'deadlines' – the plural.

Some nouns are irregular and form plurals differently. Nouns ending in 'y' end in 'ies'. Here are some examples:

singular	plural
story	stories
agency	agencies
army	armies
supply	supplies

Nouns ending in 'is'

Nouns ending in 'is' become plurals ending in 'es'. This phenomenon is quite rare, but the nouns do appear in academic writing:

Thesis = theses

Other irregular plurals

Some nouns exist in English that do not follow the usual rules when forming plurals. The plural of 'index' is 'indices', but there are other nouns ending in '-ex' that form normal plurals ('sex', for example).

It is important to remember that the verbs you use must 'agree' (that is, take the correct form) for the noun or nouns you are using. Some nouns are singular, but refer to a collection of multiple things. Sometimes this results in mistakes in essays.

Think about, for example, the noun 'group'. Group is a singular noun, even though a group will have several members. The same applies to 'community' or 'organisation'. Remember to double-check whether your noun itself is plural or singular, and make sure you use the correct form of the verb.

The following two sentences would be incorrect:

✗ The group are committed to raising awareness of human rights violations in Burma.

✗ Members of the group is committed to raising awareness of human rights violations in Burma.

The mistake made in the first sentence is surprisingly common. When you proofread, make sure your verbs agree with your nouns. The same applies to pronouns; this is discussed later in the chapter.

The correct versions would be:

✓ The group is committed to raising awareness of human rights violations in Burma.

✓ Members of the group are committed to raising awareness of human rights violations in Burma.

Effective noun use

Beyond making sure that you get the grammatical rules around nouns correct (capital letters for proper nouns and correct use of plurals; errors with these are easy to fix), the main issue around using nouns is to make sure that you use nouns that are specific and simple.

Nouns offer an area where you can demonstrate a varied vocabulary; at the same time, however, you do not want to go to extremes in using odd nouns just to avoid repetition.

Nouns are most effective when there is no alternative word type: in academic writing, especially, where abstract nouns are commonly discussed, sentences can contain large numbers of nouns. This can make writing seem very formal. A balanced mixture of nouns and verbs – which are, as you'll learn, action words – works well.

The following extract, for example, features several nouns that come from verbs. Using the verbs would make the sentence more effective and give it more impact. In the 'common mistakes' chapter, this issue, called 'nominalisation', is discussed in more detail. This essay is about the management of a small business.

> ✘ The day-to-day operating of the business is conducted under the oversight of a small team. Although employee morale is reasonable, a recent review of operations conducted by the executive group found inefficiencies in the small team's planning.

These points can be expressed in a more simple, direct way by replacing some of the nouns with verbs. Here, 'operating' is being used as a noun. 'Oversight' is a noun that also comes from a verb: to oversee. Additionally, 'review' can be a noun or verb; here it is a noun. Finally, 'planning' is a noun here.

A better example might be:

> ✓ A small team oversees how the business operates on a day-to-day basis. Although employee morale is reasonable, the executive group recently reviewed operations and found the small team was planning inefficiently.

Favouring verbs over nouns has made for a clearer extract; it has also allowed me to rearrange some of the sentences to be simpler.

Most subject-specific terms will be nouns. There is a difference between excessive use of complex, formal jargon and appropriate use of nouns associated with the topic your work discusses.

Verbs

Verbs are 'doing' words or 'action' words. Rather than naming things, verbs tell us what is *happening* within a sentence. Put simply, sentences usually consist of nouns carrying out various actions (verbs) to, with or at other nouns.

There are many different kinds of verbs (if you are interested in following them up, look up 'intransitive' verbs, 'transitive' verbs, 'regular' verbs or 'auxiliary' verbs; you'll soon find many other kinds!). Understanding the differences between them, however, is not vital to write assignments simply and effectively.

Here are some examples of verbs written in their 'infinitive' forms. This is a grammatical term that simply means the verb is prefixed by the word 'to'.

to write
to investigate
to study
to examine
to develop
to emphasise
to conclude
to undermine

Unlike nouns (except for plurals) verbs change depending on the context they're being used in. Grammar books written in many different languages often demonstrate how to 'conjugate' a verb correctly – that is, put it in the correct form for the appropriate noun – with a layout like the one below. I have taken the verb 'to examine' as my example. This list only covers the *present* tense; the next chapter discusses the *tense* of a verb in more detail.

Infinitive:	To examine
First person singular:	I examine
Second person singular:	You examine
Third person singular:	He/she/it examines
First person plural:	We examine
Second person plural:	You examine
Third person plural:	They examine

Both the 'second person singular' and the 'second person plural' are included for the sake of completeness. Verbs in the English language do not change if the second person is being used to address one person or a group – both are 'you', and the verb form is the same. This is often included in verb conjugation information because some languages do differentiate between the two.

Here is an example of the same kind of thing, but for the *past* tense. The verb is 'to conclude'.

Infinitive:	To conclude
First person singular:	I concluded
Second person singular:	You concluded
Third person singular:	He/she/it concluded
First person plural:	We concluded
Second person plural:	You concluded
Third person plural:	They concluded

You'll notice how simple the English past tense seems there. Unfortunately, many of our verbs are irregular and do very different things – try and do the same with the verb 'to write', for example!

In any case, verbs are where the action happens. As you'll find out later, the tense of a verb tells us when the action happens. Together, verbs and nouns make up a great deal of the writing you will do.

Effective verb use

Sentences with clear, powerful verbs often read effectively. This is because verbs, by their very nature, evoke a sense of action, of things happening. They tend to be less formal than nouns.

Like nouns, verbs work best when used specifically. The English language has a wide range of verbs that mean very specific things, or provide a different sense of a similar idea; think of the difference, for example, between 'grow' and 'develop'.

Use simple, clear, effective verbs. Sentences that contain effective verbs give a clear, powerful sense of action. Vary your verbs where possible, but again, don't go overboard.

Key Point

Remember that 'to be' is a verb. It is a common verb in many kinds of writing, and in speech – but it is *especially* common in academic writing. Academic writing tends to focus on abstract concept and ideas more than other types of writing. When ideas are being discussed, the verb 'to be' tends to come up frequently. You will often write sentences containing words like 'is', 'are', 'will be', 'was', 'have been' (all forms of the verb 'to be').

Verbs must 'agree' with the nouns that are carrying them out. In the examples you've seen over the last few pages, you've seen that verbs take different forms for plural nouns. Obviously, the agreement of verbs must remain *consistent* throughout a sentence.

In this example, due perhaps to sloppy proofreading, one of the two verbs doesn't agree with the noun 'committees'.

> ✗ These committees attempt to promote diplomacy and raises the profile of charitable groups around the world.

Because both 'attempt' and 'raise' are verbs being carried out by the same noun, they should agree in the same way:

> ✓ These committees attempt to promote diplomacy and raise the profile of charitable groups around the world.

If another noun is introduced, double-check that each verb agrees with the noun carrying out that action. In the following example, 'raise' is agreeing with 'projects', and so takes a different form:

✓ These committees attempt to promote diplomacy and their projects raise the profile of charitable groups around the world.

Some other issues to consider include: avoid using the verb 'get'. It tends to be vague and informal; many other languages do not have the equivalent of such a vague verb. 'Get' is often paired with another word or phrase, but you can usually find a single, more effective verb to replace this.

Some example replacement phrases for verb phrases including 'get' are shown here (there are many others, but this demonstrates the idea):

Get bigger = grow

Get away from = escape

Get better = improve

Get worse = worsen/deteriorate

Get closer = approach

Get less important = diminish

As you can see, an informal phrase like 'get less important' reads much more effectively as 'diminish'. In cases where you can't replace a 'get' phrase, 'become' is often a suitable replacement.

This idea can be applied in another situation: where the verb in your sentence is made up of several words, it is known as a 'verb phrase'. In many cases, these are necessary and appropriate; the problem described in the previous sentences was that verb phrases including the word 'get' are made informal by the informal nature of that verb.

However, *if possible*, replacing a verb phrase with a single verb is a way of making your verbs more powerful and effective. Replace a verb phrase with one verb if there is a verb that means the same thing; and the single verb is itself appropriate, simple and clear.

Do not spend too much time on this exercise while writing early drafts; in a way, it is a more 'advanced' technique that will improve as you practise. Here are a few pairs of sentences; the first in each contains a verb phrase (in **bold**), and the second a single verb replacement for the verb phrase (also in **bold**):

✗ A common theme in Robertson's later novels is the idea of characters **chasing after** people who abandoned them in the past.

✓ A common theme in Robertson's later novels is the idea of characters **pursuing** people who abandoned them in the past.

✗ The programme of treatment the GP has **told the patient to take** seems **not to deal with** potential psychological problems from the injuries.

✓ The programme of treatment the GP has **recommended to the patient** seems **to ignore** potential psychological problems from the injuries.

✗ In the 'methodology' section, Reese does not **provide reasons for** his decision to conduct a qualitative study.

✓ In the 'methodology' section, Reese does not **justify** his decision to conduct a qualitative study.

These examples demonstrate that, while the use of verb phrases is often appropriate (if sometimes bordering on informal), using single verbs makes a sentence clearer and more effective. Remember that verbs are where the action happens, literally!

In the last example, for instance, the phrase 'provide reasons for' includes a verb ('provide'), a noun ('reasons') and a preposition ('for'). 'Justify' is one verb that replaces all of this. Another possibility might be 'explain': it is up to you as the writer to decide which potential replacement words fit best, depending on what you mean.

In the following, final example, two alternative replacement verbs give the sentence a slightly different meaning. First, read the original sentence, with its verb phrase in **bold**:

✗ Several recent news reports (*The Times*, 2010; *The Observer*, 2011) have highlighted how much time MPs **take up** travelling.

Two possible replacements for 'to take up', in the sense of 'time', are: 'to spend' and 'to waste'. It might depend on the nature of the news reports that the essay references, but the sense of these two sentences is very different:

> ✓ Several recent news reports (*The Times*, 2010; *The Observer*, 2011) have highlighted how much time MPs **spend** travelling.
>
> ✓ Several recent news reports (*The Times*, 2010; *The Observer*, 2011) have highlighted how much time MPs **waste** travelling.

The second sentence clearly expresses a negative view, suggesting time spent travelling by MPs could be better spent doing something else. The first, however, is more neutral. Depending on the rest of the paragraph, it might even be expressing a *positive* view – suggesting that the stressful nature of the job, including extensive travelling, means MPs should be respected.

Finally, the 'tense' of a verb – the form a verb takes depending on *when* the action happens – is also an important consideration. Because it affects a whole sentence, however, this is discussed in the next chapter.

Pronouns

Pronouns are used in place of nouns. Again, there are various kinds (demonstrative pronouns, indefinite pronouns, interrogative pronouns, and more) and again, being able to define each kind is not vital to write good essays.

They are very common in all kinds of writing, and in speech.

If you had to refer to 'the author of the study' twenty times on one page, or you were writing an essay about Sigmund Freud and so referred to him throughout an essay, or needed to keep mentioning a particular political ideology like 'neoliberalism', and used these names or nouns in full, your writing would be incredibly long-winded and difficult to read.

The same goes for any kind of writing, and for speech. Once you've made it clear to the reader what you're talking about, or what noun is being discussed at a particular point in your work, you can use pronouns. Here are the most common:

I

You

He

She

It

We

The following words are technically different types of pronouns, but are still used to refer to a particular noun:

Which
That
This
These
Those
His/hers/its
Many
Both

Note that pronouns, with the exception of 'I', do not begin with capital letters even if they are replacing proper nouns; unless they are starting a sentence, as usual.

Here is a paragraph with no pronouns: the noun is used in every case. It is obvious how often pronouns are needed, in writing and in speech.

> ✗ The problem with Johnson's study is that at no point in the study does Johnson address any of the criticisms made by other authors of similar studies. Johnson's study, in fact, repeats many of the mistakes found in recent research in this area, and Johnson's conclusions are therefore doubtful. However, some of Johnson's conclusions in Johnson's study do support common themes in research from around 20 years ago (Deckard, 1982; Ribauld, 1984).

Clearly, this is a confusing paragraph. Nearly every noun is repeated. Here is the same paragraph, with pronouns – and other techniques to repeat nouns – used appropriately:

> ✓ The problem with Johnson's study is that at no point in it does Johnson address any of the criticisms made by other authors of similar studies. The study, in fact, repeats many of the mistakes found in recent research in this area, and his conclusions are therefore doubtful. However, some of Johnson's conclusions in the study do support common themes in research from around 20 years ago (Deckard, 1982; Ribauld, 1984).

Note that I did not use a pronoun every time I could have. In the next section, you'll see how important it is to make sure pronouns are used sparingly and clearly.

Effective pronoun use

Because nouns are very common in academic writing, pronouns are commonly needed to refer to them.

Do not overuse pronouns. It is better to repeat a noun if this will avoid confusing your reader. If you are in doubt as to whether a reader will understand what your pronoun means, then use a noun instead. Keep the distance between nouns and their associated pronouns as short as possible.

Always make sure that it is clear which noun a pronoun is replacing. This paragraph contains several pronouns; most of them are potentially confusing:

> ✗ Project management as a field, and area of expertise and research, suffered in the 1970s as it lost standing in the eyes of the public, which witnessed several high-profile projects fail. These were mostly situated in the public sector; this was compounded because at this time it was suffering from a poor reputation anyway. It only began to improve after the introduction of new methodologies and more positive stories in the news. Some of them are still prominent today and organisations in the field work very hard to promote efficient project management; they seem to be enjoying some success.

Most readers would make some sense of the paragraph above, and the general theme is fairly clear. 'Some sense' and 'fairly clear' are not good enough in academic writing, however! If your reader has to work to understand a paragraph, your point will suffer – as will your marks.

Let's take a look at the problems.

The first pronoun is 'it', halfway through the first sentence. Because it has followed several nouns – 'project management', 'field', 'area of expertise and research', 'the 1970s' – the reader has to *assume* 'it' refers to 'project management'. Again, hoping your reader assumes correctly is not ideal. Not only has the pronoun followed several nouns, it is many words away from the noun it refers to. This makes the problem worse.

Next, 'which', shortly afterwards in the sentence, is also problematic. The reader might think 'the eyes of the public' witnessed projects fail, which is reasonable. They might also wonder if 'the 1970s' witnessed projects fail – this is a more informal expression, and as such it is best avoided. Either way, the fact that 'which' does not *clearly* refer to a noun is a problem.

Then problems arise with 'these' at the start of the second sentence. 'These' projects seems to be the most reasonable (and correct) assumption, but because very soon more pronouns – 'this' and 'it' – appear that probably do *not* refer to the projects, the reader cannot be sure. This is another problem to note: if several pronouns appear close to each other, and refer to different things, your reader might be confused.

The pronoun 'this' which I've just mentioned ('this was compounded … ') does not seem to refer to a noun at all – unless the writer is using 'this' to refer to the 'standing' in the eyes of the public. However, this noun was so far back in the sentence, a reader has to go back and double-check what the writer means. Again, if your readers have to do this, your overarching argument will suffer badly.

Similarly, 'it' ('it was suffering from a poor reputation') might refer to 'project management' or 'the public sector'. In fact, the author means the 'public sector', and is attempting to demonstrate that, because the public sector already looked bad, high-profile failures within it were even more damaging. As such, here is a valid, clever point damaged by potential confusion in the reader.

The third sentence begins with another 'it'. The noun preceding it is 'reputation', which is fine. The lack of clarity around the previous 'it', however, might make the reader think twice about this assumption. As you can see, problems earlier in the paragraph are now damaging the reader's experience further on. Here, 'it' could refer to the very first noun 'project management'.

In the final sentence, it is not clear whether 'some of them' refers to 'new methodologies' or 'positive news stories'. Use of the phrase 'some of them' presents the same problem – made worse by the fact that a new noun, 'organisations', has also been mentioned, adding a third option.

Below, I've adapted the paragraph. I have proceeded step-by-step, asking myself what each pronoun referred to, and made sure it is clear in the writing each time. Sometimes this has meant changing the order of words, repeating a noun or removing pronouns. I've also added a new noun ('damage') to make a pronoun more effective.

> ✓ Project management suffered in the 1970s, losing standing as a field and an area of expertise and research in the eyes of the public. The public witnessed several high-profile projects, mostly situated in the public sector, fail. This damage was compounded because at the time the public sector was already suffering from a poor reputation, which only began to improve after the introduction of new methodologies and more positive stories in the news. Some of these methodologies are still prominent today and organisations in the field work very hard to promote efficient project management; this promotion seems to be enjoying some success.

In some cases, above, I have added nouns to the paragraph. They are prefixed with a pronoun to demonstrate to the reader that I have control over the writing, and that I am deliberately linking ideas.

For example, 'damage' has not appeared until 'this damage' begins the third sentence. Because I use 'this', the reader knows I am referring back to something, and the noun 'damage' tells the reader I am describing the sequence of events in the earlier sentences as damaging. My point is made in an effective way.

Similarly, at the end of the paragraph, I write 'this promotion'. Earlier, the verb 'promote' was used. I link the noun to the verb with the pronoun 'this', and it becomes clear that I am shifting focus from 'the organisations' to the work that they are doing, with its results. In this manner, using a pronoun *and a verb*, where the verb has not actually been used already, can be very effective.

If a writer uses techniques in a *deliberate* way, the confidence shows in the writing, and the reader is more likely to follow an argument. In the first example, there was a sense that the writer did not have control over the paragraph, and that the reader had to make assumptions.

As well as leading to actual confusion, this lack of control can lead to the reader losing confidence in your writing. Confident writing leads to confident reading.

The final piece of advice on pronoun use is: make sure your pronouns agree with the nouns they replace.

This is often quite simple: in the following example, a masculine pronoun is used for a clearly feminine noun:

> ✗ Mother Teresa has suffered criticism, too. He has been attacked in several books.

That is at one end of the spectrum, and mistakes like that one should be identified during the proofreading process.

Here is another mistake, from an essay about the costs of healthcare; this mistake is slightly less obvious:

> ✗ A committee, made up of seventeen senior officials and ex-officials from the NHS, was established by the Minister for Health. The committee's report, after a lengthy editing process, was published in 2007. These suggested the financial state of the health system was deteriorating (DoH, 2007).

The final sentence begins with a confusing 'these', which is a plural pronoun. The most obvious noun this pronoun refers to is 'committee's report', which is singular. The reader, then, might think 'these' is referring to both 'the committee' *and* its 'report'.

While this is feasible, this is an example of how a grammatical mistake has forced the reader to question exactly what the author means – this is never a good thing.

Additionally, academic sentences should be *specific*. The author should make it very clear exactly where the suggestion has come from.

In conclusion: use pronouns sparingly but appropriately; ensure they agree with their respective nouns; make sure that your reader knows what these respective nouns are; finally, don't be afraid to combine pronouns with nouns where this will reinforce your point.

Articles

There are three 'articles' in English. This is relatively simple, compared to other languages. These three words fall into two categories. They are:

> ✓ Definite article: the
>
> ✓ Indefinite article: a, an

These words precede nouns. Note that there are many cases when *no article* is used.

Although the words themselves are short and simple, correct use of articles is quite difficult to explain. Even people who speak English every day use articles incorrectly when they write. The rules for using them are also difficult for people learning the language.

To give you an idea of how important articles are, here is a sentence with all the articles removed. It comes from an essay discussing complications associated with alcoholism:

> ✗ Problems arise due to phenomenon named after doctor who discovered it; Korsakof's condition leaves patient in dangerous situation with only slim range of treatments open to doctor caring for patient in hospital setting.

It is immediately apparent that articles play an important role in making sentences clearer. Instantly, the reader can tell that something is 'missing'.

The basic rules for deciding which article to use are given below. If you struggle with articles, I suggest finding a grammar book for people learning English as a foreign language.

'An' is used before words beginning with a vowel *sound*. 'A' is used before words beginning with a consonant *sound*. In most cases, this will simply be indicated by whatever letter a word begins with – but not always. So, use 'a study' but 'an investigation'; use 'a dissertation' but 'an in-depth dissertation'; use 'a European' but 'an hour-long European studies seminar'.

To determine which article to use, or whether no article is needed, ask the following questions of the noun. You'll see that some answers end the sequence of questions, while in some cases you'll ask them all:

- Is the noun specific or non-specific?

    - A 'specific' noun will be one that a reader could identify in particular: perhaps it has been mentioned already; perhaps it is obvious from the context.
    - A 'non-specific' noun will not be specifically known to the reader. The noun might be being mentioned for the first time. Alternatively, the noun is a group, or general category, or a non-specific member of a general category.
    - Quite often, nouns move from non-specific to specific as the author mentions them once then continues to discuss them.
    - Specific: 'The'.

Non-specific: ask the next question:

- If non-specific, is the noun countable or uncountable?

    - To determine whether the noun is 'countable' or 'uncountable' try putting a number in front of it. Most common nouns are countable. Note that the issue at this point is not whether the noun is plural or not, just whether it *can* be counted. For example, you can write: three essays; two concepts; both elections.
    - The following are examples of uncountable nouns: Oxygen; sand; French; clothing; rice.
    - Uncountable nouns tend to include: groups of similar items/some abstract ideas/ languages/areas of study/food.
    - Uncountable: no article.

Countable: ask the next question:

- If non-specific and countable, is the noun singular or plural?

    - Singular: a/an.
    - Plural: no article.

Note that nouns being owned by another noun (the possessive case) do not take an article. You could not write:

> ✗ Toyota's the annual report...

but instead

> ✓ Toyota's annual report...

or

> ✓ The annual report issued by Toyota...

In the last example above, the possessive is not being used.

To demonstrate these rules in action, here are a few more example sentences; note the articles used in each one:

> ✓ The studies conducted by Sorenson between 1980 and 1987 demonstrate her focus on bullying in a primary school.
>
> ✓ Primary schools can be sites of complex, unpredictable bullying behaviour (Sorenson, 1985).

In the above example, 'the studies' are specific in the first sentence, but only appear in referencing in the second. We are also told, in the first, that Sorenson conducted her study in 'a primary school' – because this is being mentioned for the first time, the reader does not know it as a specific noun yet. If the school were mentioned afterwards, the definite article would be used.

In the second sentence, 'primary schools' is being used in the general sense, and is a plural, so no article is used. The same goes for 'sites'.

Here is another pair of sentences, comparing Marxism as a sociological perspective to its more political side; again, compare the article use in each.

> ✓ The consensus in more recent commentary (Harlin, 1986; Etienne, 1988; McMillan, 2002) makes this suggestion: as a critical perspective, Marxism has, arguably, performed more strongly than it has as a political ideology.
>
> ✓ Damage done to the ideological aspects of Marxism by historical events over the past 100 years has not had as much of an impact on its analytical power.

The first sentence mentions a specific 'consensus', easily identified by the reader because of the referenced research. 'Suggestion' does not take an article, but is preceded by 'this', which serves a similar purpose. Marxism is one critical perspective of many, and as such 'critical perspective' takes the indefinite article. The same logic applies to 'a political ideology'.

A noun begins the second sentence: 'damage' is used in the general sense, and is uncountable, so has no article. The specific nature of 'ideological aspects' makes the definite article necessary. 'Historical events' is a general group, countable and plural, so takes no article. '100 years' is specific, because the reader is explicitly told these years are the *last* 100; hence the definite article. The 'impact' is being mentioned for the first time, and as such is classed as non-specific. The 'analytical power' is being owned by the possessive 'its', so no article is used.

In both cases, 'Marxism' as a proper noun takes no article.

Modifiers (describing words and phrases)

'Modifiers' are words and phrases that provide a reader with more information or detail about parts of a sentence. They include adjectives and adverbs, which are describing words that have their own sections, below.

Some modifying phrases contain additional 'factual' information, or extra subject–verb–object arrangements. To show examples of this kind of modifier, that is not descriptive in a qualitative way, I've highlighted the modifying phrases in the next two sentences. The more descriptive modifiers are discussed afterwards.

> ✓ *Hamlet,* **written in various versions between 1600 and 1623**, seems to represent a shift in Shakespeare's tragic mood.
>
> ✓ **Although extensive research has been conducted on the disease in theory**, in practice, cancer remains a potentially traumatic and life-changing experience for any patient.

These modifiers are not the focus of this section. They are additional parts of a sentence, around the main subject–verb–object, that often appear, and often serve as a useful tool to vary our sentence structure. Descriptive modifiers are more of an issue.

I want to make a general point about descriptive language: academic writing does not, and should not, include extensive use of it. Remember that academic writing is objective. It is based on logic and reason: the writer uses evidence and gathers research to construct an argument that convinces readers of the writer's conclusion.

Descriptive writing is often more about *subjectivity*; how the writer sees something and chooses to describe it.

Key Point

Some subjects studied at university do involve more subjective elements. I should know; I studied English and Creative Writing. Similarly, how can a Film Studies student analyse a film if they cannot use descriptive language?

Clearly, descriptive language does have a very important place in certain subjects. You are not likely to be describing artwork, for example, simply using adjectives and adverbs; you will be expected to go further than that.

There is a difference between the sentences in the first box, and the sentences in the second (all come from arts-based subjects):

✓ Shelley's later poems, including the two this essay focuses on, build on the themes of class struggle prevalent in the country at the time.

✓ Several critics (Hawthorne, 1979; Mitchum et al, 1987) have pointed out that 20th century literature has produced two distinct visions of totalitarianism: Orwell's *1984* and Huxley's *Brave New World*.

✓ The film's opening shot, which pans slowly across an expanse of desert, immediately and effectively establishes the sense of isolation that grows stronger as the film continues.

✓ This prose poem was written after several attempts at writing a short story failed; the power of contemporary prose poetry, with a similar tone, is clear in works by Oakley (1999), Horley (2003) and Sukhvinder (2005).

✗ Most of the characters in the play are very realistic.

✗ The first half of the album is clearly more enjoyable and emotional because the lyrics seem to be more heartfelt.

> ✗ To reach the courtroom in the last episode's final scene, the two main characters must run very quickly.
>
> ✗ Every poem in this anthology has a wonderful rhyme scheme.
>
> ✗ It is a terrible shame that Walker died before he could write another novel.

Even though the sentences in the first box contain descriptive language, and – in almost all of them – the writer is making a point of their own about their subject, they are all appropriately written for an essay.

Points are supported, and none of the sentences in the first box involve the writer simply describing (using adjectives and/or adverbs) an artistic work in a subjective way, according to their views.

The second box *does* contain sentences that simply assign some descriptive language to a subject. Much of this description is subjective – 'enjoyable' and 'seem to be more heartfelt', for example. These sentences are not making a particular point but just describing artistic sources. No references are used in support.

Additionally, some of the sentences just narrate or provide basic information. Pointing out that characters 'must run very quickly', for example, is of no merit unless the importance of this is made clear. Simply describing events, whether they are in an artistic or fictional source or otherwise, does not often result in marks for your essay.

In fact, these points apply to any academic subject.

Remember: although you might be studying a subject that requires you to read and discuss artistic works, you are still expected to engage in thoughtful academic discussion and support your arguments with evidence.

Studying these subjects does not force you to reduce your writing to simple description of your reading, based on your own subjective opinions.

A general rule worth bearing in mind is – the *more* descriptive the modifier is, the more important it is to justify the description with references or by building up prior evidence. In a way, this is similar to emotive language; in fact, the more exaggerated a descriptive word or phrase is, the closer it gets to, potentially, being emotive.

To demonstrate what I mean by this, look at the following examples, all taken from an essay about the modern history of Afghanistan:

The first sentence is acceptable.

> ✓ The Taliban regime in Afghanistan was deemed by many official agencies, international organisations, historians and commentators to be authoritarian in nature (US State Department, 1997; Amnesty, 2000; Parker & Reynolds, 2003).

In the above example, the modifier (an adjective) is 'authoritarian', which is describing the noun 'Taliban regime'.

In the next example, however, a stronger adjective is used; an adjective so much stronger I think the author should spend more time justifying it:

> ✗ The Taliban regime in Afghanistan was deemed by many official agencies, international organisations, historians and commentators to be authoritarian (US State Department, 1997; Amnesty, 2000; Parker & Reynolds, 2003) and even medieval in nature (Johnson, 2002).

'Medieval' is quite a strong adjective in this context, and probably needs more justification than one indirect reference. In an improved example, I give more detail about the evidence that has led me to describe the subject of the sentence in this way:

> ✓ The Taliban regime in Afghanistan was deemed by many official agencies, international organisations, historians and commentators to be authoritarian in nature (US State Department, 1997; Amnesty, 2000; Parker & Reynolds, 2003). Some journalists went as far as dubbing the Taliban's rule as 'medieval' (Johnson, 2002, p97), basing this on specific practices such as stoning (Herbert, 2004).

Similarly, here is an example of a sentence in which quite a powerful adverb (the word 'rapidly', describing the verb 'shrinking') is given support and context with additional evidence:

> ✓ After his election, President Reagan signed Executive Orders that followed through on his campaign promises, rapidly shrinking the federal government: the pace of new regulations dropped to its lowest point since 1923 (Hollis, 1992) and government spending slowed by 8%, compared with an increase of 14% over the Carter years (Crelborne, 1998).

What I am demonstrating in this example is that *I*, as the author, have chosen to describe something as 'rapid', based on the research I have done (which I have then referenced). This is the aim in academic writing – to make it clear that you are formulating your own ideas and conclusions based on your studies. The sentence is a good example of this phenomenon, on a small scale.

The chapter on conciseness and clarity discusses removing unnecessary description in more detail, but for now, note the following: words like 'very' and 'really', that can be attached to many describing words, add almost nothing to academic writing and should be avoided.

Adjectives

Adjectives are words that describe nouns.

Here are some adjectives; I've focused on examples more likely to appear in academic writing:

Intelligent

Well-founded

Explicit

Effective

Detailed

Important

Rigorous

Reflective

Effective

In the box below are some complete sentences that contain adjectives:

The case study explains that the company is **large**.

Adjective = large

Several **prominent** academics have published articles supporting this idea.

Adjective = prominent

As the previous section explained, descriptive writing is not as common in academic writing as in other kinds of writing; when adjectives are used, they should be necessary and powerful.

Some adjectives do not 'describe' in the way we think of things being described – in the sentence I've written above, after the example adjectives ('In the box below…'), the word 'complete' is an adjective, describing the noun 'sentences'.

Effective adjective use

In addition to the general points made in the preceding 'modifiers' section, which cover both adjectives and adverbs, there is something else worth noting.

At certain points, other kinds of writing might have the description of something as the *focus*. When a new character in a novel is introduced, for example, sentences or even paragraphs might be devoted to describing this person.

Academic writing is different in that this kind of simple formulation – Noun + is + adjective(s) – even expressed in a more complex sentence, is very *rare*. Simply describing a noun is usually not an advanced enough way to be using your word count in an assignment.

This kind of sentence, for example, should not appear in your work:

> ✗ The sentences in Paulson's poem *Troubled* (1993) are all incomplete.

Rather, adjectives should be used to provide *key* information as part of the flow to make other points. If describing something *is* the focus of a sentence or paragraph, the description must be supported by evidence, and the importance of the description made clear.

In the following example, the adjectives give the reader important information while the author makes several points. The adjectives are describing things 'on the way', almost.

> ✓ The incomplete sentences in Paulson's poem *Troubled* (1993) contribute by their very nature to the sense of loss, as well as making the reader feel 'unusually uneasy' (Harkin, 2000).

You've just read another good example of the author's point of view (that the sentences, which are incomplete, work towards a theme in a poem) combined with a referenced source (the author links his own conclusion with a different but related point by Harkin).

In the next example, the description is the focus of the sentence, but the reason that it is the focus is clear:

> ✓ The sentences in Paulson's poem *Troubled* (1993) are all incomplete; none of the other poems in this collection employ a technique that is so immediately visible.

Although the description is the focus here, the author has explained to the reader that there is a reason for this.

Bearing in mind this rule and the rules described in the 'modifiers' section, two other important points concern adjectives:

- As always, make sure they are *specific*. Choose adjectives carefully.
- Unless you have a reason for doing so, you should not often attach more than two adjectives to any noun in a sentence. As you've learned, most sentences in academic writing will have fewer adjectives than this, and many of them will be more 'informative' (as in the example I provided earlier, where the adjective was 'complete').

Adverbs

Adverbs are words that describe verbs. They commonly end in 'ly'. The list below shows some examples.

Rapidly

Commonly

Explicitly

Overtly

Eagerly

Although I deliberately chose to provide examples of some adverbs more likely to appear in essays, generally, adverbs are rare in academic writing.

There are several reasons for, or factors behind, this rarity. For the same reasons that adjectives are relatively rare in essays, compared with other kinds of writing (again, the subject is an important factor here), adverbs are more so; description runs the risk of being subjective and not based in fact or on evidence.

Because verbs in academic writing tend to describe very specific, particular actions, the need to provide more description about how they take place should be reduced.

Removing unnecessary description is discussed in a later chapter. For now, note that words ending in 'ly' benefit from extra investigation as you edit your work.

Effective adverb use

In addition to the guidance given in the 'modifiers' section, some additional points about adverbs are worth remembering.

Many adverbs that do appear appropriately in academic writing fit into four categories. I've listed the categories, and provided some examples of adverbs that you might consider using in each one. Adverbs that fall outside of these categories are more likely to be unnecessary:

- **Intensifying adverbs** – making a verb seem stronger, or have a larger effect
  - Examples: more; extremely; even; quite
- **Restricting adverbs** – narrowing the context of a verb
  - Examples: only; particularly
- **Hedging adverbs** – being careful so as not to jump to conclusions
  - Examples: usually; sometimes; generally; probably; relatively; perhaps
- **Additive adverbs** – signposting additional action
  - Examples: further; also

As you can see, most of the adverbs common in academic writing act as signposting language, pointing the way for the reader, rather than creating more subjective description.

Conjunctions

'Conjunctions' are small joining words. In a way, they are a very basic form of 'signposting language', which will be discussed later in the book. Conjunctions indicate, in a simple way, the relationships between different ideas within a sentence or phrase. The most commonly used conjunctions are listed below.

And
But
So
Or
Yet

Other phrases that belong to a group of slightly different conjunctions include 'either ... or ...'; 'whether ... or ...' and 'just as ... so ...'.

Effective conjunction use

Sentences in essays and assignments should never begin with a conjunction (you might see this rule ignored in other kinds of writing).

Additionally, remember that conjunctions, like other words, have specific meanings and uses. Sometimes conjunctions are used incorrectly to awkwardly stick unrelated sentences to each other.

Here is an example of this problem, which most commonly occurs with the word 'and':

> ✗ The company declared bankruptcy in 2002 and only one of the company's former executives continued to work in the field of biotechnology and his new venture became one of the sector's most notable success stories.

There are three grammatically complete sentences in the example. They are all linked only by the word 'and'. The word 'and' should be used to group related ideas, just as 'but' should be used to show that one idea excludes another, or that one idea is contrary to another.

If you find a complete sentence on either side of an 'and', you should probably just write the sentences separately.

The first 'and' in the example is unnecessary. The reader might get the impression that you are attaching ideas that come from the same topic together, rather than carefully thinking about how events, causes and consequences are actually related.

In this specific example, I think the second 'and' can remain, because the ideas are very closely linked; if the person in the example hadn't continued to work in a particular industry, his new company would not have been that industry's success story.

Prepositions

Prepositions indicate the position of, or sometimes the relationship between, nouns or pronouns.

Here is a list of the most common prepositions:

To

From

(Continued)

59

(Continued)

In

Into

Under

Above

Until

Towards

Between

Beside

Below

Before

After

With

Effective preposition use

Ensure you use prepositions carefully. Think about the difference between these two phrases:

✓ The company put measures in place **before** the audit.

✓ The company put measures in place **after** the audit.

Both sentences are grammatically correct, but their meaning is very different, and will lead to different conclusions – just because of the different preposition.

Some verbs, or verb phrases, use specific prepositions – make sure you use the correct ones. For example, you 'focus *on*', 'tend *to*', 'withdraw *from*', and so on.

As you read and research in preparation for an assignment, look at the prepositions used and the phrases they are part of. Your vocabulary will develop and your use of them will improve.

Summing up

Familiarising yourself with the types of words most common in academic writing, in order to best make use of the 'effective use' sections in this chapter, is a valuable exercise. It is more immediately valuable than memorising grammatical terms without putting the concepts into practice.

In terms of the effective use of each type of word, the consistent advice is: use the most specific, meaningful words you can to make your point; vary your vocabulary where possible, but don't write strange sentences in order to do this; and finally, when in doubt about a particular word or phrase, remove it in favour of a simpler option that you are more reassured by.

The next chapter builds on this advice to clarify how these different concepts/terms are then used in sentences. Because the different types of punctuation are important in building up sentences, I discuss punctuation in the next chapter, and not this one.

Remember that some of the ideas and potential issues mentioned here appear again in later chapters (most likely the 'common mistakes' chapter), where specific aspects of them are discussed in more detail.

Further reading

Bourke, K (2006) *Grammar: Pre-intermediate*. Oxford: Oxford University Press.

Bourke, K (2006) *Grammar: Intermediate*. Oxford: Oxford University Press.

Coffin, C (2009) *Exploring English Grammar*. Oxford: Routledge.

Crystal, D (2004) *Rediscover Grammar*. Harlow: Longman.

Hewings, M (2005) *Advanced Grammar in Use: A self-study reference and practice book for advanced students of English*. Cambridge: Cambridge University Press.

Hopkins, D (2007) *Grammar for IELTS: Grammar reference and practice*. Cambridge: Cambridge University Press.

3

Putting Sentences Together

Now that you're familiar with basic academic and grammatical conventions, the next step is to understand how to craft grammatically correct, effective sentences in your work.

Doing this builds on the rules this book has already discussed. As always, you should be aiming for simplicity and clarity.

The definition of 'sentence', provided below, is my own:

> A sentence is the smallest collection of words that makes grammatical sense and expresses a complete thought.

At the most basic technical level, remember that sentences begin with a capital letter and end with a full stop. Between that first word and the full stop at the end will be a variety of words and punctuation.

Key Point

Sentence structure is also known as 'syntax' – you might see this mentioned in your feedback; it means the same thing.

There is no fixed rule around sentence length. Reading your work aloud is a good way of gauging whether your sentences are of an appropriate length: too many pauses and they are too short; running out of breath signals that they are too long.

As a rough rule, most sentences in academic writing are between thirteen and twenty words long (excluding citations; in the Harvard system I use, for example, these numbers would exclude the surnames in brackets).

As your writing develops, and you try to vary your sentence structure, making them different lengths is a good starting point. They should still end up somewhere between the numbers suggested above, however.

First, there is a basic grammatical arrangement your sentences should follow: subject–verb–object.

All complete, correct sentences will contain what is called a 'subject' (which will be a noun) and at least one verb. Almost all sentences in academic writing contain an 'object' (a noun). This basic grammatical concept is commonly called 'subject–verb–object' for the sake of simplicity.

Remember that this idea does not supersede or negate what you've learned about nouns and other kinds of word. These are new concepts that apply specifically to sentences; you can have a list of nouns on a page, for example, but a noun can only be the 'subject' of a sentence if it is performing a certain function in that sentence.

Subject–verb–object

All sentences have a *subject*. The subject will be a noun or a pronoun of some kind.

The subject is the part of the sentence that carries out the actions happening in a sentence. The subject is the noun that 'does' the verb.

As the previous chapter explained, a *verb* is an action word.

The *object* is the noun that is having the verb act upon it; it is being affected by the action of the verb.

Here are some simple examples:

> ✓ Eisenkopf writes novels noted for their use of language to parallel the mental states of their characters.
>
> Noun = Eisenkopf
>
> Verb = writes
>
> Object = novels
>
> ✓ Although the theory has been criticized, the committee remains a recognized authority on the debate.
>
> *(Continued)*

(Continued)

Noun = the committee

Verb = remains

Object = authority

✓ The increase in the use of learning management systems in further education has resulted in higher expectations among students making the transition to university level.

Noun = The increase in the use of learning management systems in further education

Verb = has resulted in

Object = higher expectations among students making the transition to university level

Key Point

Some sentences, conceivably, could be grammatically complete with no object.

As you've been reminded, 'to be' is a verb. It is the verb in the following sentence; there is no object:

✗ This research paper is thoughtfully structured.

'This research paper' is the subject, 'to be' is the verb, and there is no object. 'Thoughtfully structured' is a modifier; it contains describing language, but no nouns.

Technically, this sentence is correct. However, as the 'modifiers' section in the previous chapter argued, this sentence is too simple for an essay. Academically appropriate sentences should not limit themselves to simply describing a noun, which is exactly what this sentence does. If a sentence has no object, it is probably doing something similar.

As such, always ensure your sentences contain an object.

As you write, edit and proofread your work, if you come across a sentence that seems incomplete somehow – this is especially noticeable if you read your assignment aloud – double-check the presence, and agreement, of a subject, verb and object.

Quite often, this sense of incompleteness comes from one (or more) of these elements being missing. It is important to remember that just identifying verbs in your sentence is not enough: verbs can appear as part of modifying phrases (in the box of three example sentences, 'has been criticized' is a verb). Your sentences must have a verb carried out by a subject and affecting an object.

For example, the next two sentences are missing different parts of the subject–verb–object arrangement:

✗ In the literature, fierce debate around the role and achievements of grammar schools in the UK.

(Missing verb)

✗ By the time the advertising campaign had ended, increase in sales of over 23% (Y.D. Industries Annual Report, 2007).

(Missing subject and missing verb)

Because the missing elements have been identified, it becomes easier to solve the problems:

✓ In the literature, fierce debate **continues** around the role and achievements of grammar schools in the UK.

✓ By the time the advertising campaign had ended, **the company had seen** an increase in sales of over 23% (Y. D. Industries Annual Report, 2007).

You have seen, therefore, how understanding the subject–verb–object concept makes it easier for you to write complete sentences, and to rectify problems with incomplete ones.

Being comfortable with the concept also provides opportunities to vary your sentence structure. In the same way that you should vary your vocabulary where appropriate, you should write sentences that vary in structure.

However, you should not do this if changing sentence structure makes the sentence potentially confusing or hard to read; in these cases, it is better to stick to a simple structure that you are sure makes sense. Similarly, you should avoid spending too much time rephrasing sentences if you have other, more important issues to resolve in your work.

Varying sentence structure is a skill you will develop naturally as you write. That said, examining the subject–verb–object arrangement of your sentences is a good place to start learning. This way, you can identify areas where you can make simple changes to improve variation.

Going through one of your paragraphs, for example, you might find that your sentences break down like this:

> ✗ [Modifying phrase] + [subject] + [verb] + [object]. [Subject] + [verb] + [object]. [Modifying phrase] + [subject] + [verb] + [object]. [Subject] + [verb] + [object].

Clearly, this is quite repetitive. You might want to think about moving the modifying phrases around, provided you can ensure the sentences are still readable and grammatically correct. Combining this technique with varying sentence length, mentioned at the beginning of the chapter, can introduce considerable and effective variety into your writing.

Finally, understanding this subject–verb–object idea is crucial to grasp the concept of the 'active' and 'passive' voices in sentences.

Active and passive

Most sentences can either be written in the 'active' voice or the 'passive' voice. Basically, the different voices refer to the order in which components in a sentence appear. The phrase 'subject–verb–object' demonstrates the active voice. In a way, 'object–verb–subject' is the passive; as you'll see, it is slightly more complex than that.

In reality, this choice only applies to some sentences. Some sentences, if swapped from active to passive, can be ridiculous; trying to switch certain passive sentences to the active can also result in some very strange writing!

The active voice consists of all or part of the sentence made up of the following formulation, which we've already seen:

> Subject + verb + object

The passive voice reverses this order. Because of this, the sentence has to be adapted slightly. The following examples will show why this must happen.

Passive sentences almost always include a form of the verb 'to be' (often 'is' or 'was') and the word 'by'. Looking at some examples, you'll understand the reason for this.

> Object + appropriate form of 'to be' + verb + subject

Here, then, are two simple examples of the same, simple sentence expressed in the two voices:

> ✓ Active: The tutor delivers the lecture.
>
> ✓ Passive: The lecture is delivered by the tutor.

Here is another example with a slightly more complicated sentence:

> ✓ Active: President Clinton and a Republican Congress achieved a balanced federal budget in 1996.
>
> ✓ Passive: A balanced federal budget was achieved by President Clinton and a Republican Congress in 1996.

These sentences are complicated by several factors. Two nouns make up the subject; the adjectives 'balanced' and 'federal' are included with the object; and the modifying phrase 'in 1996' tells the reader when the action took place. In spite of this, the active and passive voices can still be used, and still result in the order of the same parts of the sentence changing.

The active and passive voices are both grammatically acceptable. Assuming you have a choice, then, which is better?

In *most* cases, the active voice is preferable. The 'subject–verb–object' formulation is clear, logical, easy to read, and, as the word 'active' suggests, gives a sense of the action moving forward in the sentence. The passive voice seems more deliberately formal, potentially old-fashioned, and involves using additional words to make the sentence correct. If a sentence is already complex, the passive voice can make matters worse.

Only use the passive voice if you have a specific reason for doing so. Additionally, do not repeatedly write sentences in the passive voice, even if you have reasons for doing so – they will become very hard to read if used throughout a piece of work.

Use the trusty find tool to look for the word 'by' in your assignments. If this highlights an example of the passive voice, revert to the active; unless you are using the passive for one of the following specific reasons.

Removing the subject of the sentence

The passive voice allows you, potentially, to remove the subject of the sentence. The most common reason for doing this is to avoid the first person – if 'I' is the subject. An example of this might look like the following example:

- ✓ Active sentence: To reach the following conclusion, I analysed the results of various studies.

- ✓ Passive sentence: To reach the following conclusion, the results of various studies were analysed by me.

- ✓ Passive sentence with subject 'I/me' removed: To reach the following conclusion, the results of various studies were analysed.

You might also choose to remove the subject if you do not think the subject is important enough to be mentioned, or if the subject is likely to distract readers from the key point of the sentence. This choice will be yours as the writer; here, choosing to write in the passive and remove a potentially distracting subject is a specific technique available to you to make your writing more effective.

- ✓ Active sentence: McPherson-Daily published Anderson's seminal book in 1926.

- ✓ Passive sentence: Anderson's seminal book was published by McPherson-Daily in 1926.

- ✓ Passive sentence with subject 'McPherson-Daily' removed: Anderson's seminal book was published in 1926.

More rarely, you might not actually know what the specific subject of the sentence is; so you have to avoid using it.

> ✗ Active sentence: As a young man, the writer explains in his memoirs, [unknown subject] advised him to seek the help of renowned psychiatrist Dr Elsing.
>
> ✓ Passive sentence: As a young man, the writer explains in his memoirs, he was advised to seek the help of renowned psychiatrist Dr Elsing.

In the final example above, the active sentence is included for the sake of completeness and comparison with the other examples. The fact that it contains the '[unknown subject]' should make it obvious that this is not a sentence you would ever actually write. More important is the realisation that you have the passive voice available to you if you do find that you can't include the subject of the sentence.

Emphasising the object of the sentence

Choosing to use the passive voice because you want the focus or emphasis to be on the object of the sentence is, again, a decision you as a writer can make. Remember that the word 'subject' is simply a grammatical term; it's easy to get into the habit of thinking the subject of a sentence should be its most important part. This is not the case.

The following sentence, written in the active voice, is grammatically correct:

> ✓ Groups belonging to the so-called 'Christian Right' in America tend to dismiss the idea of global warming.

Just to clarify, the subject of the sentence is 'groups belonging to the so-called "Christian Right" in America'; the verb is 'tend to dismiss'; the object is 'the idea of global warming'.

In an essay discussing the various political beliefs or ideological activities of the group I've identified, this active sentence makes perfect sense. Because the subject of the sentence is the first thing the reader 'sees', there is the powerful impression that they are the focus of the sentence, carrying out various actions. The actions, the object and the additional information they add are of course very important (otherwise they would not be included at all), but it's clear what the sentence is 'about'.

What if my essay was about various aspects of the global warming debate? Or maybe my assignment discusses some problems that can hinder fund raising to raise awareness of climate change theory? Perhaps the actual group dismissing the theory is less a focus than the idea or debate around global warming itself. As a writer, you can make this decision, and decisions like this will subtly guide the reader through your argument. You can make your points more effective by ensuring the focus is where you want it to be.

If you did want to change this into a passive sentence, then, you'd write something like this:

> ✓ The idea of global warming tends to be dismissed by groups belonging to the so-called 'Christian Right' in America.

These decisions will be based on context: what you are writing about; the actual conclusion you are drawing your readers towards; where the focus of a particular part of your essay is, and so on. Read the two versions of the sentence again, and take note of the subtle difference. This difference would be made stronger in the context of a longer piece of work.

Varying your sentence structure

Although I have argued that in most cases, the active voice can and should be used, if your sentences are all very similar, using the passive voice occasionally can help you vary their structure. This idea is summarised well by Jonathan:

WHAT YOUR TUTORS SAY

'Vary the structure of your sentences in a paragraph. Don't always begin with the subject, especially if it's the same subject.' – Jonathan, History lecturer

---

Be careful following this advice. It is better for your sentences to be clear and effective, if repetitive, as you are developing your academic writing. As your skills improve, you can use various techniques to vary sentence structure.

Tense

Every verb in your essays will be written in a certain 'tense'. As well as verbs agreeing with their subjects, which you read about in the last chapter, verb tenses must be consistent and correct over the course of sentences and paragraphs.

The tense of a verb signals to the reader *when* an action happens. Because all the verbs in a sentence will be written in a particular tense – often, but not always, the same tense – the reader will know whether the events described in that sentence happen in the present, happened in the past, began in the past but are still continuing, or will happen in the future.

Using different tenses is something you probably do without thinking in speech. If English is your second language, tenses can be quite a difficult topic, because different languages handle tense differently.

Additionally, many English verbs are known as 'irregular' verbs because they do not follow the usual rules when they change tense.

To give you a better idea of the concept of 'tense', here is an example of the verb 'to write' conjugated in various tenses with the first person 'I'. 'Conjugating' a verb, remember, means making it agree with its subject. This kind of layout is very common in grammar books for learning languages:

Infinitive:	To write
Simple present tense:	I write
Simple/imperfect past tense:	I wrote
Perfect past tense:	I have written
Present continuous tense:	I am writing
Future tense:	I will write

Because the first person, as we've discussed, is very rarely used in academic writing, here is the same example, using the third person singular 'she' as the pronoun:

Simple present tense:	She writes
Simple/imperfect past tense:	She wrote
Perfect past tense:	She has written
Present continuous tense:	She is writing
Future tense:	She will write

71

The English language does, more rarely, make use of more complex tenses. Just to give you an idea of what I mean, here are a few more example phrases:

She will have written

She will be writing

A book devoted to helping someone learn English as a new language will go into detail about most of the different tenses. As well as the common present tense, English has the perfect past, the continuous, the future tense, the perfect future tense, the past historic, the conditional, and many more.

My aim in this book is slightly different, and I assume a basic knowledge of English. Because of this, I won't spend time going into this detail. Rather, I will focus on the key considerations you should be aware of when it comes to using tense in your essays.

The most common tenses in academic writing

Every time you write a verb, ask yourself the simple question: 'When is this action taking place?' If a sentence has several verbs in it, they will *often* be in the same tense, though I'll show you some examples where this is not the case. Similarly, then, most paragraphs will have a consistent tense running through them, unless there are deliberate changes in when the verbs happen.

I have provided answers to the question you should ask of each verb below. This covers the more common tenses. I then use a particular verb to provide an example of the use of these tenses.

- When does this verb take place?

  - The verb happens in the present: present tense
  - The verb is halfway through happening now: present continuous
  - The verb happened in the past, and the action is complete: simple past tense
  - The action will happen in the future: future tense

Example noun and verb: 'Journalists' (third person plural) and 'investigate'

Present:	Journalists investigate
Present continuous:	Journalists are investigating
Simple past:	Journalists investigated
Future:	Journalists will investigate

The tense of your verbs should quite clearly reflect when something happens.

Tenses in a paragraph should only change when there is a specific reason for this change. Here is an example of a sentence with several tenses being used within it:

> ✓ Because of the problems the corporation **has experienced** in the past, it now **operates** under a reformed management structure, **is conducting** a review of all its business processes, and **will implement** changes based on the recommendations of this review and others like it.

This sentence shifts from the past to the present. Then the verb 'is conducting' is written in the present continuous, because the corporation's review is ongoing. Finally, 'will implement' is an action that has not happened yet – it will take place in the future.

> **Key Point**
>
> Although, as the previous example demonstrated, tenses will change – sometimes within a sentence – it is very rare for the most common tense in an essay to shift over the course of the essay. If you are *mostly* writing in the present tense in the first half of your essay, this should not shift to the past for the second half.
>
> So if, for example, you are analysing a novel, and you decide to refer to characters, dialogue and themes in the present tense, make sure you stick to this approach throughout.

By simply asking oneself when a verb happens, you will shift tense only when necessary. Unfortunately, careless tense shifts do commonly appear in essays; they are a clear signal of a lazy approach to one's work.

There is no reason, for example, for the tense switches in this example:

> ✗ Recent problems with rioting and in the UK **highlight** a general sense of discontent and dissolution. Although youth unemployment **could not fairly be blamed** for violent crime, young people still **worry** about a lack of solutions to their problems which the government **was not dealing** with. All parties that **are involved** in this **needed to work** together.

This is the most common kind of mistake with tense changing – a mixture of present and past tenses are being used. It seems that students more easily see the difference in the future tense, perhaps because it is used more rarely.

The problems in the paragraph above would have been avoided if each verb had been examined and the question of when it takes or took place answered. At no point is a specific event that took place in the past mentioned. In the following box, I have corrected the example *and added a new phrase* that makes the past tense in 'could not fairly be blamed' appropriate.

> ✓ Recent problems with rioting and in the UK **highlight** a general sense of discontent and dissolution. Although youth unemployment **could not fairly be blamed** for the violent crimes that **took place** in 2011, young people still **worry** about a lack of solutions to their problems which the government **is not dealing** with. All parties that **are involved** in this **need to work** together.

In this corrected example, the present tense is appropriate throughout – except where I now mention violent crimes that explicitly took place in the past, in 2011. I inserted this to demonstrate, again, the power of asking when each verb happens.

Avoiding continuous tenses where possible

In the examples above, you've seen forms of the 'present continuous' tense. Continuous tenses are not confined to the present; the past continuous and future continuous are possibilities, too. A continuous tense is made up of the verb 'to be' in the appropriate form (the present, past or future tense) followed by the main verb ending in 'ing'.

Here are some examples:

He is writing
The lecturer was marking
The group will be judging

Some languages do not actually have continuous tenses – just the simple present. The simple present tense is more direct, and because of this more effective in making a point. Continuous tenses in academic writing can *almost always* be replaced with the simplest version of the appropriate tense – whether that is past, present or future.

Below are some paired examples showing this replacement in some complete academic sentences.

> ✗ Members of the public sometimes forget that senior nurses are running complex bureaucratic institutions.

> ✓ Members of the public sometimes forget that senior nurses run complex bureaucratic institutions.

> ✗ Over the next five years, small business owners in America will be experiencing the effects of Obama's regulatory and tax policies.

> ✓ Over the next five years, small business owners in America will experience the effects of Obama's regulatory and tax policies.

> ✗ In this series of novels, the author seems to be suggesting that striving for wealth should not be criticised thoughtlessly.

> ✓ In this series of novels, the author seems to suggest that striving for wealth should not be criticised thoughtlessly.

In all these examples, a simpler tense can replace a continuous verb. Continuous verbs can be found by typing 'ing' into your word processor's 'find' tool. Although changing one sentence in the manner above might not make a huge difference, excessive use of continuous tenses is a strangely common problem. Changing several sentences in this way could really make your writing more effective.

Note that sometimes verbs ending in 'ing' are appropriate and correct – like the word 'ending' in this sentence. It is the correct type of verb.

Additionally, there are times when a sense of the continuous is needed; when you need to show the reader that something is or was *in the process* of taking place.

The following example of just such a case comes from a political essay, about the 2000 Presidential campaign:

> ✗ Dick Cheney had been assigned to find a Vice-Presidential candidate for George W. Bush and was conducting a search for one when Bush chose him for the post.

It's clear in this sentence that *as Cheney was carrying out his search*, he was chosen to be Bush's Vice-Presidential candidate. If 'was conducting' was replaced with 'conducted', the reader would think that Cheney's search was complete before he was chosen. This provides a very different impression of the events.

To summarise – avoid continuous tenses, which are less effective and often unnecessary compared with simple tenses. If a continuous tense is used, there should be a specific reason for doing so.

Hedging

'Hedging' is a verb referring to a technique quite common in academic writing – nothing to do with gardening!

It does not refer to one specific technique, but an idea; 'hedging' can be carried out in various ways, but it can be summarised as a concept like this:

Academic writing, by its very nature, is sometimes tentative. The writer must jump to conclusions, or give the reader the idea that they are doing so. Academic writing often involves debate, different arguments, and different conclusions. Writers must, then, accept that although they are engaging with the debate, and becoming involved in the 'academic arena', they might not have all the answers – or all the *right* answers.

'Hedging' refers to a broad range of ways in which a writer can show that they are being tentative: they are suggesting their conclusion *might* be the right one; that *it is likely* that they are using the broadest range of evidence they can.

By hedging, a writer is, at specific points in their writing, telling the reader: 'I'm not jumping to conclusions. I'm being careful, and honest, and tentative.' As such, it contributes to the honesty academic writing should possess.

Hedging when appropriate, and learning to do so in a variety of ways, is the mark of a good writer. In a way, hedging techniques are a kind of signposting language, because they contextualise a particular point to your reader, making clear that you are being cautious as a writer.

Let's take a look at some specific ways of hedging, with examples.

Hedging can often be done using certain verbs. Here are some common words that make clear a situation is not 100% predictable or likely:

Suggests

Could

Perhaps

Seems

Might

Likely

Potentially

Possibly

Look at the difference between a sentence containing one of the above words, and a similar sentence that is not 'hedged':

✓ Results of the studies conducted by Olsen (1976) and Worthy (1984) make clear that this particular drug has risks if used in treatment over a long period.

✓ Results of the studies conducted by Olsen (1976) and Worthy (1984) suggest that this particular drug has risks if used in treatment over a long period.

Both show the author making a judgement on the strength of the evidence in their research; they are different judgements. It is more common that in academic writing, you won't be able to make as strong a judgement as the one in the first sentence.

Sometimes, hedging can be done with phrases that clearly tell the reader that the author is being cautious. Another way of doing this is to acknowledge opposing or alternative arguments where appropriate, as in this example:

✓ Though others (Crichton, 1994; Benchley, 1998) have argued the opposite, this study shows that…

Ultimately, it is your choice when to hedge, and how cautious to be when you *do* hedge – here is a version of the second sentence above with another hedging word ('might') added:

> ✓ Results of the studies conducted by Olsen (1976) and Worthy (1984) suggest that this particular drug might have risks if used in treatment over a long period.

The point to remember here is that, if you feel you need to qualify a point, it is perfectly acceptable to do so using hedging language. In fact, careful and appropriate hedging is the mark of a confident writer. As usual, look for examples of this in your reading.

Punctuation

Punctuation appears in every sentence you write. Understanding the most common parts of punctuation is vital, then. Because using punctuation is part of putting sentences together, I've included the topic in this chapter.

Here you'll find a short section on each of the *main* pieces of punctuation used in essays. Each section contains the ideas I think are most important to bear in mind when using that punctuation.

Be aware that some of the sections in a later chapter, 'Common mistakes', also discuss some issues specifically centred around the use of punctuation.

. The full stop

All grammatically complete sentences finish with a full stop. The only phrases or sentences that might not end this way would include bullet-pointed sentences, headings and other extraordinary examples.

Once you have written a grammatically complete sentence, put in a full stop. Then leave a space before you begin the next sentence. Full stops should never appear within a sentence, and are usually left out of titles, headings and subheadings.

Remember that a full stop acts as both a visual 'pause', and a similar break in a reader's head. The pause is not as long as that encountered when a new paragraph begins on a new line, but it is still significant. If you find yourself breathless when you read your work aloud, you need to break your writing down into smaller sentences – which will mean more full stops. There is nothing wrong with this.

? The question mark

Question marks end sentences that are framed as direct questions.

'Direct' questions almost always begin with a question word (like 'how', 'what', 'why', and so on).

As such, ending this example with a question mark is incorrect:

> ✗ The patient asked if this particular form of cancer was common in the United Kingdom?

Here, the sentence is one of narration; it is telling the reader that the patient asked a question, but it is not directly providing us with her question.

It is possible that this example could include a question word, but using a question mark would still be incorrect:

> ✗ The patient asked what the chances of survival for this type of cancer were?

Both these examples should take full stops, because the question is not being phrased as a question: read aloud both sentences after the word 'asked' and you'll realise the order of the words in the sentence mean these are statements.

If the direct question was provided through dialogue, using a question mark would be correct:

> ✓ The patient asked, 'what are the chances of survival for this type of cancer?'

Here, the order of the words 'what are' makes this a question. If you are ever confused about this, take the question from the sentence and read it aloud. Would you ask a question this way? Using the first example, read 'What the chances of survival for this type of cancer were'. This is not how you would ask the question (and it is not how the patient asked the question; the writer is merely describing the fact that a question was asked).

In the final example, the actual dialogue is being quoted, and it is phrased as a question would be asked.

However, dialogue will be rare in academic writing; certainly much rarer than in other kinds of writing. If you are studying something like English, you might well quote a lot of dialogue from the books you read. Other than that, however, most students will never write an essay with any direct dialogue in it.

This means that the only other circumstance that would involve the use of a question mark is the 'rhetorical question'. You may have heard this term before.

A rhetorical question is a technique, often used in speech, that is traditionally seen as a way of making the speaker or writer's point seem more powerful. It is often described as a 'question not meant to be answered'. The idea is that a rhetorical question in, for example, a political speech, will make the audience think about the answer for themselves and understand the implications of the speech.

The following box contains an example from a (fictional) political speech, showing the most common way in which a rhetorical question is used. Note that this is *not intended to be an extract of academic writing.*

> 'Time and time again, we have been given the same excuses by this government; excuses for the poor jobs market, increasing crime rates and unclear foreign policy. Who will pay the price for these failed policies?'

The rhetorical question will probably not be answered (sometimes, the person asking the question will answer it themselves, however); the aim is for the audience to ask themselves the question, and then answer it – perhaps, in this case, with something like, 'Us?', 'Me?', 'My children?'

The rhetorical question is a powerful technique in writing or speaking aimed at convincing an audience to believe something. Given that an academic essay often has the aim of making a logical argument and encouraging readers to agree with its conclusion, it is understandable that students often ask if rhetorical questions can or should be used in academic writing.

The answer is – *usually*, no. Rhetorical questions should certainly not be used frequently. They can often tempt the writer to make emotive arguments, which you have already learned should be avoided.

The other problem with the technique is that, because academic writing should be transparent, open and honest, a question that is asked but not subsequently answered will make the reader worry that you do not know the details of your own arguments or points.

My general recommendation is to avoid rhetorical questions. If your writing does lead to a question that you want to point out to the reader, then include it and make sure you answer it. If it is phrased as a direct question, use a question mark.

These similar examples (one with a direct question, one without) would be acceptable:

> ✓ Given that the evidence overwhelmingly highlights the benefits of carefully planned and consultative occupational therapy programmes, a question arises: why does the government not do more to promote awareness of occupational therapy?
>
> ✓ The fact that the evidence overwhelmingly highlights the benefits of carefully planned and consultative occupational therapy programmes raises the question of why the government does not do more to promote awareness of occupational therapy.

As long as the writer answers, attempts to answer, provides some answers, or even points out the difficulties in answering, the question they have raised, then this is perfectly effective academic writing. Note that rather than being a question 'not meant to be answered' and designed to evoke a reaction in the reader, this is the writer clearly and openly pointing out that a certain specific question must be asked in the light of, presumably, what their essay has discussed up to this point.

! The exclamation mark

The exclamation mark should, as a rule, not appear in academic writing. This is unless you are directly quoting text that contains an exclamation mark. For example, if you are writing about a book, or poem, and cite a passage from the text, include the punctuation as it is in the original. Beyond that, you'll almost never see this punctuation mark used in academic writing. Your word processor's 'find' tool, as always, can be helpful here. Just type '!' into the search bar. It is unlikely that you will have used this punctuation without being aware of it. Note that this is one of the academic conventions I don't follow in this book.

, The comma

The comma is a common, important and useful piece of punctuation. However, they are often overused, and incorrectly used – especially in academic writing.

The chapter on 'common mistakes' contains more detail on this point, but for now, I'll make this point: commas should not be used to separate grammatically complete sentences, but just to divide clauses. Don't make your sentences over-long by excessive comma use – most sentences shouldn't contain more than three commas, and this should not happen often: one or two is fine. If your sentences routinely contain three or more commas, think about breaking them down into smaller parts with full stops and some rewriting.

: The colon

The most common use for a colon is to signal the beginning of a list of words or phrases. The items in the list will be separated by commas or semi-colons, so the list will look something like this:

> ✓ The spread of 'globalisation' has consequences beyond the economic, affecting many other phenomena, including: terrorism, the spread of infectious disease, political upheaval and cultural identity.

The colon can also be used within sentences if the first part of the sentence poses a problem, or raises an issue, and then the second part of the sentence, after the colon, is a direct response to it. The colon should not be used for this purpose too often, but this is a good way of occasionally varying your sentence structure.

Here is an example of this kind of colon use, where the second part of the sentence is a direct 'reply' to the first part.

> ✓ More recent research (Collins, 2002; Kendall & Hepburn, 2007; Randall et al, 2007) has consistently highlighted a particular trend: homophobic bullying in schools is decreasing.

; The semi-colon

The semi-colon is slightly rarer than some of the other punctuation in this chapter. It is also harder to understand how to use effectively. Here I outline one of the simpler uses for the semi-colon, and provide an idea of another, more advanced way of using it. Note that if you are unsure, you can avoid the semi-colon entirely; there are always other ways of doing the same thing the semi-colon does.

The simplest use of the semi-colon is to separate items in a list, where the items are made up of more than one word. The items in the list might be whole phrases of varying length, and they might contain commas themselves. In a complex sentence that might already contain other commas, separating the list items with commas might confuse the reader.

Here is an example of such use. Note the colon, indicating the start of the list, and the phrases within the list, divided by semi-colons.

> ✓ The umbrella term 'Weapons of Mass Destruction' (WMD) refers to several distinct types of weaponry: nuclear weapons, also labelled 'strategic' WMD because of their capacity to inflict large-scale damage; biological weapons, also dubbed 'strategic'; radiological weapons, another category of 'strategic' WMD; and chemical weapons, which are often called 'tactical' WMD, because their capacity to cause damage beyond the battlefield, or over a wide area, is more limited.

Although the list itself is made up of only four items, the additional information about each item makes it necessary to clearly divide them.

Semi-colons can also be used to divide parts of sentences. Think of them as a 'pause' more substantial than a comma, but not as final as a full stop. Elsewhere in the book I discuss the problem of 'comma splicing', where commas are used to separate grammatically complete sentences. You can use semi-colons to do this. If you have two complete sentences, and the second is so closely linked to the first that you think this link should be made clear, separate them with a semi-colon.

You can see an example of this in the box below.

> ✓ There seems to be a consensus that if election debates are to have more of an effect on the views of voters, real reform is needed; a new format is often mentioned as a potential starting point.

If you're in doubt about this, avoid semi-colons and just use two separate sentences. Additionally, don't try to use several semi-colons to separate several sentences: stick to two at most.

( ) Brackets/parentheses

Some referencing styles make heavy use of brackets – the Harvard and Vancouver styles in particular (see the chapter on referencing). Other than that, they should not be used excessively. A rule of thumb is: if you remove the part of the sentence in brackets, the sentence should still make sense – grammatically, and in terms of actual content. Brackets can be used to provide additional information that is not *vital*, but potentially useful to your reader. Given that academic writing involves focusing on a series of specific, well-chosen points, you should not frequently be giving the reader 'extra' information. If you read part of a sentence that is in brackets, and decide the information is very important, try using commas in place of the brackets; or write a separate sentence that deals with the necessary content.

[ ] Square brackets

Square brackets have a particular purpose as part of referencing. They're explained in more detail in the referencing chapter.

- The hyphen/dash

Although they usually look almost identical, the hyphen and the dash are, technically, two different pieces of punctuation. To keep things simple, however, note that both are usually considered too informal for academic writing. As such, they are best avoided. Note that this is a convention I ignore in this book. When hyphens are used in academic writing, they tend to appear *inside* words; they join certain types of nouns together, or add a 'prefix' to the start of a word to change its meaning.

' The apostrophe

The apostrophe has three main purposes: to replace missing letters in contractions; to indicate directly quoted portions of referenced work; and to indicate the 'possessive' – that is, to show that one noun owns another.

Contractions have been covered in an earlier chapter, but I'll recap the material here. Direct quoting is a part of referencing more generally, and is included in the referencing chapter. The possessive apostrophe is covered here. The apostrophe is often misused in all kinds of writing; this is unfortunate, because the rules are easy. Make the effort to learn them, and you shouldn't have any problems.

As discussed in the 'basic conventions' chapter, contractions consist of multiple words joined together and shortened by removing letters.

Here are some examples of contractions, as a brief reminder. The apostrophe indicates where the missing letters would be if the words were written out in full.

Wouldn't = would not

She's = she is *or* she has (this should be clear from the rest of the sentence)

Should've = should have

As the earlier chapter made clear, contractions should *not* be used in academic writing. They are very common in less formal kinds of writing and in speech.

In a way, this fact makes it easier to focus on the other roles of the apostrophe, because all the apostrophes in your assignments should be 'possessive' apostrophes, or used as part of referencing.

A 'possessive' apostrophe is used when you are making clear that someone or something (a noun) *owns* another thing (whether a concrete or abstract noun). The letter 's', known as the 'possessive s', is also used here.

The 'possessive s' is of course obvious in spoken English, because it can be heard. The apostrophe that goes with it, however, can't be heard; this means using it correctly is something only necessary in *writing*. Perhaps this is why it is often misused.

When one noun owns or possesses another, an apostrophe and the letter 's' are added to the end of the owner. If the owning noun already ends in 's' (this might be because it is plural, though this is not the only reason), the easiest option is to add an apostrophe alone to the end of the noun. (Some books and tutors might add an apostrophe as well as an additional 's'. Either option is correct, but I think that the double 's' looks confusing and is better avoided.) If there are several owners named separately, whether singular or plural, an apostrophe and letter 's' are added to the end of the *last named owner*.

Each of these cases is shown as an example below:

The committee's report

Dr Jones' report

Jones, Ryan and Smith's recommendations

Let's look at some examples of the possessive in actual sentences.

✓ Robertson's theory, explained in detail in his article for the controversial September 2009 issue of *Modern Science*, has its admirers and critics.

85

The example contains several things worth noticing. The possessive 's', along with the apostrophe, has been used correctly in 'Robertson's theory'. Robertson, a person and as such a proper noun, owns a theory (an abstract noun). This is not a contraction; no letters are missing.

> ## Key Point
>
> When you come across apostrophes in your work, it is easy to check whether you have used a contraction (which you'll need to remove) or a possessive (which you'll need to confirm is correct). Try replacing missing letters or words where you've used the apostrophe. In this example, I can't say, 'Robertson is theory, explained in detail…' or 'Robertson has theory, explained in detail…' As such I immediately conclude that this is a possessive – and that it is correct.

This is all relatively simple, which is why it is unfortunate when marks are lost through lack of attention to detail here.

The example goes on to mention something else that belongs to Robertson – 'his article'. The possessive apostrophe and letter 's' are *not* used with pronouns (as discussed, words that replace nouns). This is the same in speech. It would be incorrect to write:

> ✗ …in his' article for the…

When a pronoun is the owner in a possessive, do what I've done in the example; don't use an apostrophe:

> ✓ …in his article for the…

Here is another example, just to reinforce the point. Imagine that full example sentence was the second in a paragraph, and that Robertson and his theory had already been mentioned. This means we can use a pronoun for 'Robertson'. As such, the beginning of the sentence would change:

> ✓ During the last few years, a new way of conceptualising progress in biosciences, has evolved, originating in various works by Peter Robertson. His theory, explained in detail in his article for the controversial September 2009 issue of *Modern Science,* has its admirers and critics.

As you can see by comparing the two examples, possessive pronouns do not need apostrophes or the possessive 's'.

Finally, both examples contain one of the most problematic words I come across in assignments. The problem is an important and common one, but it doesn't need to be. That is why I'm going to make it a 'key point'! First, let's see what someone else has to say about this...

WHAT YOUR TUTORS SAY

'Its and it's always catch students out. The simple rule is not to abbreviate; then it is impossible to get it wrong. It's easy!' – Simon, Computing lecturer

---

I'm not as pessimistic as Simon – this issue doesn't 'always' catch students out. However, it does happen too often. Simon makes the same point I have made. If you are taking care to avoid contractions, you will never use the word 'it's'; if it does appear in your work, then it must be incorrect.

The fact that a tutor mentions this as a key grammatical concern shows that your tutors do expect you to have an understanding of grammar and to proof-read for 'small' mistakes carefully; and they see this mistake far too often!

Key Point

First, there is no such word as:

✗ its'

If you find this in your written work, *remove it.*
There *is* such a word as:

✓ it's

However, it must be a contraction – the contracted form of either 'it is' or 'it has'.
You already know that contractions should *not* be used in academic writing. Logically, this leads to a simple conclusion: *the word 'it's' with an apostrophe should never appear in an academic assignment.*

> ### Key Point
>
> Sometimes a situation arises where you've used a word that is actually a singular word that *feels* like a plural, because it has several parts. For example, the word 'group' is a singular. If I was writing about the revisionists as a group, I would write 'Most of this group's theories tend to oppose...'. When you are writing in a possessive context, think carefully about whether your noun is plural or singular. Think about the difference, for example, between 'staff' (singular) and 'members of staff' (plural).

Further reading

The 'further reading' section at the end of the next chapter includes books and other resources that you'll find useful when writing sentences, paragraphs and whole assignments.

4

Putting Paragraphs Together

Now that you have an idea of how to construct sentences, we will look to the next largest section of academic writing – the paragraph.

To begin, I'll provide a working definition of what a paragraph is:

> A paragraph is a logically ordered sequence of grammatically complete sentences. These sentences express one idea or make one point in considerable detail. All the sentences in a paragraph should contribute to this idea or point. They might potentially expand on it, but will not deviate from it.

Many of the principles behind putting sentences together also apply when forming paragraphs, which should be clear, simple and to-the-point.

It seems reasonable to assume that a paragraph made up of clear, well-written sentences will also be clear and well-written. To an extent, this is true; provided you bear in mind the ideas discussed in the previous chapter, as well as other key ideas in this book (the referencing guidelines, for example), you'll find that your paragraphs are likely to be similarly effective.

There is more to constructing good academic paragraphs, however, than just writing decent sentence after decent sentence. This chapter will look at some of the ideas that make up the 'more' in this context.

In technical terms, the guidelines for laying out paragraphs on the page tend to be similar across subjects and institutions. They can only vary slightly.

Commonly, a new paragraph begins on a new line and is indented (which means that the first sentence begins further to the right than the normal page margin). Some tutors will ask that you also start each new paragraph with an extra space (that is, an empty line) before beginning the new paragraph.

Although this is probably the most that will be expected of you, it is always worth checking with your tutors or in your course handbook just to be sure. Also remember, of course, to make the appearance of your paragraphs consistent – if you are indenting them, and that's all you are doing, make sure you indent *every* paragraph!

Most academic paragraphs average between 45 and 75 words; going by the suggested figures for sentence length, given in the previous chapter, this means paragraphs will usually consist of between three and six well-developed sentences.

There will be many that fall outside this guideline, but if you are *consistently* writing shorter paragraphs, you should check that you are expressing your ideas fully enough; and if you are *consistently* writing paragraphs that are longer than this, take a look to make sure you are breaking your points down in a suitable way.

Paragraphs should discuss one particular topic, or make one point; the topic or point is then reinforced with the relevant detail, references, examples, and so on. Paragraphs should not address a wide array of subjects; nor should they make points that are too brief. I'll show you some examples over the next few pages.

You should be able to summarise a decent academic paragraph in *one* sentence (try doing this, informally, with friends). If you really struggle to do this, the paragraph probably needs some additional work.

While it depends on the assignment you've been asked to complete, and at what stage you are in the assignment, *most* academic paragraphs should contain a few well-chosen references. Effective referencing, including appropriately working our sources into our essays, is discussed in a separate chapter.

While individual sentences might be perfectly clear on their own, when you start to think at the paragraph level, you should consider a powerful tool available to you: 'signposting' language. This is not a technical grammatical term, but is generally used to refer to a wide range of words and phrases that help the reader follow your argument.

Signposting language can make clear why one point follows its predecessor; how points are or are not linked; the relationship between cause and effect; and much more. This might sound very complex, but when you see some examples, you'll realise that you use signposting language all the time, often without knowing it!

I'll discuss signposting language in more detail later in the chapter; I mention it here because it is a good example of a technique that becomes more effective, and necessary, in paragraphs.

WHAT YOUR TUTORS SAY

'Attention to detail indicates that you care about how you present yourself.' – Mariann, Biosciences tutor

---

Mariann's point is a very important one – she is suggesting that your tutors will be looking for effective practice in *all* aspects of your writing. An excellent essay written as one long paragraph (to take an extreme example) will betray the fact that the author has not paid attention to the detail of how paragraphs are arranged. This will undermine the whole piece of work.

Take Mariann's advice – use the opportunity of an assignment to present yourself well! This also brings me on to my next point…

Key Point

Sometimes students bring me essays that are excellent in many respects – *except for the paragraphing*. It is quite common for essays to not be divided into paragraphs at all, or divided a handful of times every few pages. More rarely, I see very short paragraphs that seem to start and finish randomly throughout the piece of work.

Sometimes, students don't seem to attach much importance to the idea of paragraphing correctly. Paragraphs, however, are vital (if they weren't, they wouldn't be in this book). First, they have a strong cosmetic impact on your reader, the first time they see your work – even if it's just a glance.

Like you, tutors marking your work will feel their hearts sink if they see pages and pages of text not divided into paragraphs at all. It means that well-written points can get 'lost' on the page, losing their impact.

Writing that has been almost 'randomly' divided up into very short paragraphs, or paragraphs that vary wildly in length, can lead your readers to think that you are being lazy in breaking your work into its main points. Alternatively, they might wonder if you are not even fully aware of what your main points are. This is a very damaging way for your readers to be thinking!

Ultimately, paragraphs help your reader to see how you've arranged your points. They also help *you* ensure you've discussed a point in enough detail, and to assess whether you have presented enough of a counterargument. Paragraphs are as helpful a tool for a writer as they are a device for the reader.

Signposting language

A key technique that comes into its own in paragraphs is the use of 'signposting language'.

Signposting language is not an 'official' grammatical term. Additionally, it has quite a broad meaning. Signposting language refers to words and phrases that give your reader a sense of the direction your argument is going in. That is, these phrases 'signpost' the way.

While grammatically correct sentences and paragraphs can make effective points on their own, signposting language adds an extra level to an essay, providing the author with the chance to tell the reader various things.

Signposting language can say: this thing happened because of these other things; this idea opposes that one; these ideas reinforce each other; this idea is related but different; the essay's focus is shifting at this point; now the essay is going to highlight some opposing arguments; the essay is reaching its conclusion; all these things and many more.

Before looking at specific examples of signposting language and what they are used for, compare the following two example paragraphs, from an assignment discussing the role of technology in education. They say similar things, but one is more effective than the other.

✗ The debate around the proper role of online learning remains highly charged, despite massive advances in the technology that can be involved in it. Beyond the often emotional nature of a debate so close to the hearts of academics, many conclusions are apparent in the research. Parker (2003), Maxwell & Roberts (2006) and JISC (2010) maintain that the benefits of 'well-deployed' technology-enhanced learning (Maxwell & Roberts, 2006, p307) can be exponential.

✗ Meyer (2005) and Holmes (2008) argue that more traditional forms of teaching are still highly valued. A wide range of research (Jackson, 2004; Wyle, 2006; Tomlin, 2007) reaches conclusions somewhere in-between. Over the years, students themselves have become increasingly vocal (NUS, 2011) in demanding what Meyer disparages as 'the best of both worlds' (p198). It seems that involving oneself in this discussion involves careful dissection of the arguments.

✓ The debate around the proper role of online learning remains highly charged, despite massive advances in the technology that can be involved in it. Beyond the often emotional nature of a debate so close to the hearts of academics, **however**, many conclusions are apparent in the research. **On the one hand**, Parker (2003), Maxwell & Roberts (2006) and JISC (2010) maintain that the benefits of 'well-deployed' technology-enhanced learning (Maxwell & Roberts, 2006, p307) can be exponential.

✓ **On the other hand**, Meyer (2005) and Holmes (2008) make the **contrasting** argument that more traditional forms of teaching are still highly valued. **Alternatively**, a wide range of research (Jackson, 2004; Wyle, 2006; Tomlin, 2007) reaches conclusions somewhere in-between. Over the years, **additionally**, students themselves have become increasingly vocal (NUS, 2011) in demanding what Meyer disparages as 'the best of both worlds' (p198). It seems, **then**, that involving oneself in this discussion involves careful dissection of the arguments.

The addition of a few well-chosen phrases (highlighted in bold) makes the writing more effective. Each instance of signposting language in the second version of the extract has a specific meaning, and is being used carefully. As with any other word or phrase, signposting language should be used in a precise and appropriate way.

Look back over the paragraphs in this book, and you'll see that I regularly use signposting language. Without these words and phrases, academic writing would be a series of statements. The reader would be forced to construct links between these statements themselves. Remember that effective academic writing creates a logical argument; a progression of points building to a conclusion. In doing so, academic writing does not rely on the reader creating this progression themselves; signposting language helps the reader follow this progression more closely.

Signposting language can be used to highlight the relationship between specific points, as it does in this example, from an essay discussing the 2004 US Presidential election:

> ✓ Some analysts blame Kerry's loss on the tendency of his campaign to focus on biography (Underwood, 2005; Johnson, 2006). **Alternatively**, a different school of thought suggests that important social issues on the ballot in several states drove up the number of Republican voters (Ryan, 2007).

In the above example, the word 'alternatively' makes it clear that a *different reason* for the *same outcome* is being proposed.

Additionally, signposting language can signal to the reader where the essay itself is going, as it does in this example from later in the same politics essay:

> ✓ The range of arguments explaining the outcome of the 2004 election, and the lack of *overwhelming* evidence for any one suggest, **in conclusion**, that John Kerry suffered defeat because of a multitude of reasons.

The key to effective signposting is to do so very specifically. Don't just sprinkle these words and phrases through a piece of work as you proofread; make sure you think through how to use them appropriately as you write.

Here are some of the most common phrases, as well as the context in which you'd use each one:

Presenting contrasting ideas/arguments

by contrast

in contrast to

however

on one hand/on the other hand

rather

conversely

in comparison

compared to

Providing different reasons/evidence that have the same result or making a similar point

alternatively

likewise

again

also

additionally

similarly

equally

in addition

Setting up a conclusion

in conclusion

finally

overall

lastly

Summarising evidence

to summarise

in summary

overall

Demonstrating cause and effect

despite

because of

Providing examples

for example

for instance

namely

such as

Emphasising a point

indeed

in fact

furthermore

moreover

Being more specific

in particular

in relation to

more specifically

particularly

in terms of

In addition to the above phrases, it is worth bearing in mind that almost any sentence or part of a sentence can act as a 'signpost', by creating direction for the reader.

In the following extract (from an essay discussing a director's filmography), for example, a different kind of phrase is used:

✓ Rogers has said in various interviews (*Time*, 1980; *Newsweek*, 1985) that his films tend to reflect his political views overtly and explicitly. **These statements give the audience an idea of how to interpret his most recent work, *Exodus*.**

The phrase in bold is essentially telling the reader that what will follow are the various ideas involved in interpreting a particular film.

In this way, as you write paragraphs, you will use the common signposting phrases mentioned above; it is also, however, worth thinking about how other phrases can prepare the reader for the progression of your argument. If you need to tell the reader what is coming next, do so.

Topic sentences and staying on topic

Almost every paragraph of good academic writing in an assignment will contain a 'topic sentence'. In fact, the first sentence in a paragraph is often the topic sentence. It's certainly easiest, when getting started writing essays, to write them at the beginning of your paragraph (you can always, if appropriate, move them around later). Topic sentences can also finish a paragraph. Less commonly, you can find a topic sentence somewhere in the middle of a paragraph.

So what are topic sentences? The clue is in the name. Read the following example paragraph, from an essay about the Mormon religion:

> ✓ Mormonism continues to have a rapidly developing, evolving public profile. The religion is not only growing in numbers of followers (Fyne, 2010), but is sometimes hotly debated in the American media. Recent popular books (Krakauer, 2006; Jefferies, 2009) have presented both criticism and investigation into Mormons, particularly in the USA. Additionally, high-profile adherents have been advancing through the political arena in recent years, notably Democratic Senator Harry Reid and Mitt Romney, twice a presidential candidate.

One sentence in this example acts as a kind of summary of the others. If not a summary, it certainly identifies the main theme or idea the paragraph is discussing.

I gave you a hint in the beginning of this subsection – it's the first sentence. The other sentences are all grammatically correct, and could stand alone. Imagine the paragraph without that first sentence – it would just be a series of factual statements. With this topic sentence, the writer has made a clear, strong point (about the increasing public awareness of Mormonism) and then reinforced it with other sentences that provide a range of appropriate evidence.

Topic sentences usually either act as summaries, or point out a key theme or idea. They can work in different ways, depending on the nature of the paragraph. In that first example, we had a topic sentence making a point, and the other sentences providing the evidence that, in the writer's view, proves that point.

In this next example, from an essay on scientific research, the topic sentence is doing something slightly different:

> ✓ Early in his first term, President Bush issued a controversial ruling about stem cell research. The debate about climate change continues, and several scandals have rocked the consensus in recent years. The long-term effects of a serious oil spill will

> make themselves clear over time after the BP spill off the gulf coast. Awareness of the moral dangers associated with the intertwining of bioethics, nanotechnology, and similar fields, have moved from otherworldly science fiction into serious discussion. Clearly, science as a broad field is still filled with vigorous, potentially emotional debate, and the future contains serious challenges that science both poses and hopes to address.

Here, the topic sentence is the last one. Again, the others provide the *detail* and consist of effectively written, linked facts. It is the topic sentence that explicitly makes the link. The other sentences are *examples* of the main idea in the topic sentence: that debate and challenges exist in contemporary science.

The writer has skilfully picked varied examples, so the other sentences are equally important – but it is in the last sentence that the writer's own strength in grouping these examples shows. Note the signposting language: after all of these examples, the writer is confident enough to say to the reader, 'clearly...' which works more subtly, perhaps, than a more obvious alternative – for instance, a phrase like 'these examples prove that...', which would also perform a similar purpose.

It is worth taking a look at one more example of a topic sentence before I summarise their potential purposes and importance. This paragraph is from an essay about a British poem:

> ✓ Although the theme has clearly been established in the first stanza of the poem, the second stanza really develops the theme of growing distance between the aristocratic and poorer classes in England. This can clearly be seen in the phrase…

Here, you can see a strong topic sentence that is clearly identifying the writer's next focus: the *second* stanza (verse) of a poem. The signposting word 'although', and the rest of the first phrase, also make a distinction between the ideas in previous paragraphs, and the ideas to come in the following sections.

An effective topic sentence is *not* a brief statement of fact – you as a writer should be demonstrating some way of engaging with the topic. The topic sentence above, from the essay analysing a poem, is a good example of this.

Topic sentences should *not* be brief value judgements that are not backed up with evidence in some way (simply labelling something associated with the topic/subject 'good' or 'bad'). Topic sentences should also be very specific and about some particular aspect of the topic.

Poor topic sentences often make it harder for you to know how to develop the rest of your paragraphs.

The next box contains examples of the kinds of sentences that would make very poor topic sentences. Beyond that, these sentences would be ineffective wherever they appeared in an assignment.

> ✗ The band's most groundbreaking album was released in 1982.
>
> ✗ George Galloway belonged to the Labour Party before he left to form Respect, the party he now represents in Parliament.
>
> ✗ The effects of climate change are terrible.

These examples could quite easily come from more journalistic or popular writing. The first two are just statements of fact. The writer is not setting up an interesting paragraph. Try to make it obvious that you as the writer are present in your topic sentences. By this I mean that your topic sentences are a great opportunity to present the critical details that form your argument.

The third example seems dangerously subjective and far too brief for an academic point. To say something, particularly a broad and complex theory like climate change, is 'bad' (or 'good') without justification or detail is not academically appropriate. This topic sentence does not provide such justification *or*, crucially, introduce it.

It is true that the rest of the paragraph that this topic sentence comes from might include examples of the effects of climate change. However, this would result in a paragraph made up of a weak, subjective value judgement, followed by simple factual statements. These statements might be referenced, but this would still be descriptive writing, not academically engaged writing.

The chapter on critical thinking and referencing provides more information on this. For now, be aware that the focus of academic writing is not on facts.

If anyone could look at an encyclopedia, news report or internet post, and find versions of your topic sentences, or all the facts within them (the second example in the box is a perfect example of this), you have a problem. Your topic sentences are too descriptive and factual.

Instead, topic sentences should do something more. They should prove to the reader how you are engaging with a topic and reaching your own conclusions *based on your research.*

Here are some stronger topic sentences, on the same topics:

> ✓ At the time, critics saw the band's 1982 album as a failure, though the fact that it is seen more positively now highlights the band's presaging a shift in attitudes to music.
>
> ✓ George Galloway's departure from the Labour Party can be seen as a move that highlights his own political shift, or the Labour party's; perhaps both.
>
> ✓ While climate change, broadly, has had many effects on the world, some positive and many damaging, some key consequences can be identified by examining the effects and their differences across continents.

If you've written a poor topic sentence, the best remedy is probably re-examining the entire paragraph, rather than simply replacing the sentence with a better one. That said, you might find, on examining the paragraph, that this is all that's necessary. I'm simply suggesting it's best not to *assume* this simple replacement is the solution.

The point I am making is that your assignment briefs should provide plenty of scope to build an effective, logical argument based on your engagement with your research material. This is more than simply reciting facts.

As such, think about the main point you want to make in a paragraph. Put that specific point into a topic sentence in a way that will also allow you to develop or add more detail in the following sentences. The revised examples offer a much better opportunity to include references in a way that proves that the author has actually engaged with their reading, not just learned facts about a certain topic.

Sometimes, topic sentences will include signposting language, or act as signposts themselves. For example, if I've written a paragraph explaining how climate change has affected developing countries comparatively more negatively than other countries, I might write this topic sentence at the start of the following paragraph:

> ✓ However, some of the effects of climate change, and the climate change debate, could be seen as affecting the developing world in a more *beneficial* way.

Again, by making it clear that I will be presenting a different group of examples from my research, this topic sentence is demonstrating that I have engaged with what I have read.

This next example, from an English essay, is also acting as a kind of signpost. Here, the writer is moving on from discussing a novel, to focusing on a compilation of short stories – both by the same author.

> ✓ By contrast, the post-colonial themes so strongly established in all of Willis' novels up to this point, do not seem to provide the same undercurrent in the collection of short stories.

Both examples contain some of the signposting phrases I've mentioned elsewhere in the chapter. They also, as good topic sentences, make a clear and specific point that provides plenty of potential to go into more detail and develop the point.

Trying to identify the topic sentences in the paragraphs you read, and developing the skills to write them effectively, are valuable exercises. Writing good topic sentences will also have a positive impact on your paragraphs as a whole. This is because an effective topic sentence tends to push an author towards more thoughtful, detailed and engaging paragraphs.

Key Point

Even if topics sentences don't contain signposting language as I have defined it, or clearly mark a change in an argument's direction (the sentence above, beginning 'By contrast', is a good example that does this), topic sentences act as a kind of signpost in themselves.

They tell the reader what your paragraph will be about, and give an idea of the specific detail they can expect to read.

Key Point

A student I was teaching once got the wrong idea. We had discussed essay structure in a previous session. In your essay's introduction, you often explicitly tell the reader what the essay contains. Main topics and their sequence will be outlined as part of the introduction.

This student applied a similar logic to her topic sentences – she saw them as miniature 'introductions' to the paragraph. This led to her writing topic sentences like, 'This paragraph will be about Shakespeare's sonnets'.

As you can imagine, this led to some very strange paragraphs and many wasted words. Don't think of topic sentences as little introductions: they are very much at the heart of the topic. Because of this, they make specific points *about* the topic.

As you have seen, they can be identified and used to make clear to the reader what key point you are making; but they are not introducing the point, they *are* the point.

We've discussed how long paragraphs should be, and the fact that they make one point, in detail. This specific point is controlled by a topic sentence. You'll learn more about referencing later on, but for now note that almost every paragraph you write should have one or two well-chosen references in it to back up a point.

How can you get a sense of how the sentences beyond your topic sentence remain related to that original point? Here is a quick exercise you can do. At first it might seem a little confusing, but you'll learn to do it very quickly and eventually, you won't have to do it at all. By this point, you'll instinctively know how 'unified' your paragraph is – that is, how appropriately linked your sentences are.

Essentially, you'll be assigning each sentence in a specific paragraph a number. If you find it hard to number a particular sentence, you know you've identified a potentially problematic paragraph.

Similarly, if you end up counting too far (that is, have too many numbers), you should examine which points need whole paragraphs of their own, with the additional detail necessary.

After providing the instructions, I'll give an example by working through a paragraph of my own.

Staying on topic – checking your paragraphs

- Start by reading the topic sentence. This might be the first sentence, of course. The topic sentence is number 1.
- Then read the other sentences in the paragraph in order. Each of them will get a number.
- If the sentence is providing more detail about the topic sentence, directly, it gets labelled 2.
- If the sentence is developing or providing detail about any number 2 sentence it is labelled 3.
- If the sentence is developing or providing detail about any number 3 sentence it is labelled 4.
- If the sentence is developing or providing detail about any number 4 sentence it is labelled 5
- ...and so on.

Therefore, if you find a particular sentence is very difficult to number, you've identified the fact that you're going off topic, or haven't thought through the points you're making, and how they fit together.

Ask yourself if you need to include the problem sentence at all. Is the information in it necessary? If so, it might form a new paragraph that needs more detail itself. If you don't need to discuss it, or decide it's irrelevant, remove it.

If you find yourself routinely counting too high, you are probably discussing a topic in too much detail for one paragraph. Your topic is *too broad* for one paragraph. Again, break the work down. Think about what you *need* to discuss; pull out the details and, potentially, form new topic sentences and paragraphs.

Again, remove what isn't relevant and provide enough detail about the points you need to make.

There is no definitive rule, but I usually recommend that most healthy academic paragraphs should, in addition to a topic sentence, consist of four or five sentences, all labelled 2 or 3. The occasional 4 is alright, but should be rare. Going further than 4 is probably a problem.

With this exercise, you can actually gain considerable insight into your writing. Interpreting the results from each paragraph can tell you a lot.

Think about it: if your paragraph goes **1, 2, 3, 3, 3, 3** then your topic sentence is probably finding its foundation in the sentence you've labelled 2; your number 1 (topic sentence) might be weak, or not specific enough. Can you remove it? Or perhaps you've gone too far developing the point in sentence 2 and need to rework the paragraph to focus more on what's in the topic sentence?

The more used to this exercise you get, the more useful the conclusions you can make. Just to give you an idea before we look at an example, common number arrangements, with the topic sentence at the start, are:

1, 2, 3, 2, 3 or 1, 2, 3, 3, 2 or 1, 2, 2, 3, and so on.

Let's put this into practice. Here is a paragraph from an essay about the history of surgery. First, you can read the paragraph as it appears in an essay. Following that, I number each sentence according to the instructions I've provided.

> ✓ A key aspect of surgery handled with relative ease during modern procedures, but that posed serious problems even into the 20th century (Ambrose, 1982), is control of the patient's bleeding. Before modern developments, patients commonly bled to death before or during surgery; this has been discussed in detail by Cahill (1973) and Jameson (1987). Early methods of controlling bleeding included cauterisation and tying blood vessels with ligatures. 'Cauterising' wounds (sealing them with heat) was painful and dangerous, while the ligature method left the patient in danger of infection. This was particularly dangerous until the nature of infection was fully understood (a momentous discovery, chronicled adeptly by Atkins (1953)). Modern surgery has seen the introduction of successful, relatively simple blood transfusions, carried out from the early 20th century.

✓ A key aspect of surgery handled with relative ease during modern procedures, but that posed serious problems even into the 20th century (Ambrose, 1982), is control of the patient's bleeding. **Topic sentence = 1**

✓ Before modern developments, patients commonly bled to death before or during surgery; this has been discussed in detail by Cahill (1973) and Jameson (1987). **Directly related to #1 = 2**

✓ Early methods of controlling bleeding included cauterisation and tying blood vessels with ligatures. **Directly related to #1 = 2**

✓ 'Cauterising' wounds (sealing them with heat) was painful and dangerous, while the ligature method left the patient in danger of infection. **Directly related to #2 = 3**

✓ This was particularly dangerous until the nature of infection was fully understood (a momentous discovery, chronicled adeptly by Atkins (1953)). **Directly related to #3 = 4**

✓ Modern surgery has seen the introduction of successful, relatively simple blood transfusions, carried out from the early 20th century. **Directly related to #2 (second sentence) = 3**

✓ **Paragraph numbering: 1, 2, 2, 3, 4, 3**

Now that the final numbered sequence for the example is clear, it is possible to draw some conclusions from the process and the numbers themselves.

First, I had no major problems actually numbering any of the sentences. The only slight issue arose when numbering sentences three and six (in the order they appear in the paragraph). I realised it was hard to determine whether they related more to the topic sentence or the second sentence, which I have numbered **2**. As you can see, I came to a conclusion, but this issue suggests that the first two sentences of the paragraph make a very similar point.

I might think about reducing these two sentences into one, ensuring the references from both, and the main points from both, were combined.

The other notable concern, then, is the presence of a number **4** in the paragraph. The sentence prior to it provides detail about the two early surgical procedures (cauterization and ligatures). The sentence labelled **4** then provides yet more detail about a different topic – the nature of infection. This was raised in the previous sentence, but seems out of place.

Finally, this sentence highlights a 'momentous discovery'. If a discovery is particularly momentous, should it really be tucked away in a long paragraph, appearing very briefly? Should it seem like an additional piece of information vaguely linked to the broad essay topic, but not the specific point the paragraph is making? I think the number **4** sentence is problematic, and should be removed to form a topic sentence of its own. I can use signposting language to make sure that the links between paragraphs are clear.

An extract with these improvements made might look like this (note that the second paragraph should not be considered complete; it would continue in a full essay):

> ✓ Before modern surgical developments, even into the 20th century (Ambrose, 1982), patients commonly bled to death before or during surgery (Cahill, 1973; Jameson, 1987); this highlights the importance of controlling a patient's bleeding, now handled with relative ease. Early methods of controlling bleeding included cauterisation and tying blood vessels with ligatures. 'Cauterising' wounds (sealing them with heat) was painful and dangerous, while the ligature method left the patient in danger of infection. This was particularly dangerous until the nature of infection was fully understood (a momentous discovery, chronicled adeptly by Atkins (1953)). Modern surgery has seen the introduction of successful, relatively simple blood transfusions, carried out from the early 20th century.
>
> ✓ Beyond the problems it caused when ligatures were used, the danger of infection was an additional, serious issue at nearly every operating table until the momentous sequence of discoveries that led to it being understood. Atkins (1953) provides a definitive account of this critical discovery that has had far-reaching implications for all surgical procedures.

As you can see, a simple numbering exercise has actually helped me locate issues with the focus of my writing that might not have been so obvious otherwise. The exercise also highlighted a superfluous (unnecessary) sentence; by keeping its key points, but putting them in an existing sentence, I am making my writing more concise. This is a later chapter's major concern!

Key Point

Remember, this exercise still works with paragraphs that do not begin with the topic sentence (that is, sentence number 1). You just have to remember to start with the topic sentence when numbering each one – because the topic sentence is always labelled 1. Because of this, this exercise also forces you to make sure your paragraph contains a clear topic sentence.

Bearing this in mind, it's not uncommon to see number arrangements like **2, 2, 2, 1** or **2, 3, 1, 2, 2**. Remember, though, that as you start out writing essays, it is easier to aim for your topic sentences to be either the first or last sentence in a paragraph. Working them into the middle is more difficult (but you can vary the rhythm and 'feel' of your paragraphs by doing this occasionally).

What, why, when

Other useful exercises you should be able to do with each paragraph you've written include summarising them in one sentence in an informal way – perhaps aloud with friends. Similarly, a friend should be able to read a paragraph you've written and summarise it in one sentence too.

You might see a similarity between your summary and your topic sentence, but a summary should take into account the whole paragraph.

This summarising is the '**What**' question – **what** is this paragraph saying?

For example, an out-loud, casual summary of the medical paragraph you've already seen is included in the box below, underneath the paragraph:

> ✓ Before modern surgical developments, even into the 20th century (Ambrose, 1982), patients commonly bled to death before or during surgery (Cahill, 1973; Jameson, 1987); this highlights the importance of controlling a patient's bleeding, now handled with relative ease. Early methods of controlling bleeding included cauterisation and tying blood vessels with ligatures. 'Cauterising' wounds (sealing them with heat) was painful and dangerous, while the ligature method left the patient in danger of infection. This was particularly dangerous until the nature of infection was fully understood (a momentous discovery, chronicled adeptly by Atkins (1953)). Modern surgery has seen the introduction of successful, relatively simple blood transfusions, carried out from the early 20th century.
>
> Summary:
>
> ✓ 'This paragraph is about the problem of patients bleeding to death during operations – this problem has existed until quite recently, and various methods were tried to deal with it before blood transfusions became mainstream in the 20th century.'

If you struggle to summarise your paragraph in a sentence, it might be that the paragraph is tackling too many points and needs to be broken down. Alternatively, you might not actually understand (or believe) what you have written, which is a worrying sign!

You should also be able to explain – again, an informal approach is fine – **why** you need this paragraph in your essay. That is, why your reader needs to be aware of, or consider, the idea in the paragraph. This is the '**Why**' question.

Doing that, for the same example paragraph, might sound something like this:

> ✓ 'This paragraph is important because the reader needs to know that this specific, major problem in surgery was not properly solved until the 20th century, and that old methods posed dangers rather than really solving it.'

Finally, you should be able to explain the need for this paragraph to appear **at this point in the essay**.

Sometimes your 'why' answer might include some of this answer too, or even answer this question completely as well. If you do need it separately, though, this is the '**When**' question.

So for our example, you might say:

> ✓ 'It's important for my reader to know this now because it's part of a sequence about main considerations in surgery. As well as being important in itself, it's the one that allows me to make a link to the next major part of the essay – the danger of infection, and how understanding it was a big part of the history of surgery.'

Key Point

My examples above have been informal, and written as if they were spoken. The aim of this exercise is not to make extensive notes answering these questions – certainly not until you identify issues. Then you can make notes to make sure you know what you need to do to improve your work.

If anything, these questions don't work as well if they are made too formal. Once, during a session I was teaching, a student asked if he should write down the answers to these three questions for each paragraph in her essay.

The answer is no. Even if you are not working in groups, you can still maintain an informal state of mind as you write and think through these questions. If you genuinely can't summarise why you've written a paragraph, or what your paragraph is saying, in a simple and quick way, you've identified an issue.

Further reading

Greasley, P (2011) *Doing Essays and Assignments: Essential tips for students*. London: SAGE Publications.

Greetham, B (2008) *How to Write Better Essays*, 2nd edn. Basingstoke: Palgrave.

Hopf, C (2012) The Power of the Paragraph [online]. Available at: http://vimeo.com/44666462 (accessed 26/08/2012).

Peck, J and M Coyle (2012) *The Student's Guide to Writing: Spelling, punctuation and grammar*, 3rd edn. Basingstoke: Palgrave.

Ramage, J (2009) *The Allyn & Bacon Guide to Writing*. Harlow: Pearson Longman.

5

Critical Thinking and Referencing

WHAT YOUR TUTORS SAY

'It is good to make use of other sources. Just be sure to accurately reference them.' – Simon, Computing lecturer

Simon's quote captures the key idea of this chapter. You are expected to make substantial use of the reading and research you've done. However, you must make it clear to the reader when you are doing so. You might be an excellent writer, but your essays will never get top marks if you don't bring other ideas from your field into them.

Key Points

Here are some key points I'll make in this chapter. I've made some of them already:

- This is not a book about referencing, and how to do it in a technical sense, though I will discuss the key principles of referencing, and show you examples of common referencing styles.

(Continued)

(Continued)

- I'm writing about referencing to show you how crucial it is to know why and how we are expected to use our reading, and other people's work in our essays.

- Engaging with your reading, and all the research you do, is called 'critical thinking'. The level of engagement with what you read should increase as you progress through your studies. For example, you should show evidence of more careful critical thinking in a second year essay than a first year essay, and so on.

I've split this chapter into two – referencing, and critical thinking. The referencing section deals with the 'technical' aspect of integrating other sources into your work – what it looks like on the pages of your work. I'll then provide a basic definition of 'critical thinking' and provide examples showing effective critical thinking in action.

Remember that the topics aren't really 'separate'. Try and consider them together. They are two crucial parts of the same thing: showing your reader that you have researched the literature, sources and ideas surrounding your topic; and you are now presenting your own ideas in the context of what you've learned.

Referencing

When we present the reader with evidence from our reading or research we must *reference* it.

Referencing is a broad term, and usually means *all* the things you must do to provide information about your sources; referencing, therefore, involves doing several things. Here is my definition:

Referencing is a system used to make clear to the reader when you are bringing ideas, words, quotes, illustrations, concepts or anything from other sources into your own assignments.

There are many referencing systems, also known as referencing styles. Some are almost identical, some vary more widely. Their aim is always the same: as stated above, to point out where you are using other sources. Whether you mention a radio interview, a computer game or a journal article, you'll have to reference these sources in a certain way, according to a certain system.

WHAT YOUR TUTORS SAY

'Develop a system for recording your resources used. When writing notes on the articles you've read, head your notes with the date, title, author and source of the material. Write this in the reference style required for the academic bit of work. And keep them all in one place!' – Alice, Occupation Therapy lecturer

Alice's point is important because, as you might be realising, referencing means collecting and using an awful lot of information. Just take a look at the reference lists at the backs of your textbooks, or the footnotes on their pages! Make sure, as Alice says, you save your information in a practical way that works for you. The librarians at your university don't like getting frantic questions about which book a certain quote is from – mainly because it's very hard for them to help you in a situation like that! *Always* make a note of the information your referencing system uses when you are studying or reading.

Think of referencing as how you make clear to the reader *what* sources you use. Critical thinking is the approach you take when analysing your sources – *how* you use them.

Remember that, a few paragraphs ago, I mentioned that 'referencing' referred broadly to a range of different things. Before talking briefly about the different systems, let's look at what those things are.

In most referencing systems, referencing is made up of:

- a 'reference list'/a list of 'works cited', which contains your 'full' or 'long' references **at the end of your assignment**

and

- a 'citation' of each source, which might be 'direct' or 'indirect' **on the page of your assignment when you use that particular source**. As such, you'll have citations appearing throughout your work, and some sources might be cited several times.

Key Point

You may have heard of, or seen, the term 'bibliography'. Sometimes you might provide one at the end of a piece of work. So what's the difference between a reference list and a bibliography?

The two are often confused, with good reason. They usually *look* the same; they use the same referencing style/system.

(Continued)

109

(Continued)

A reference list/works cited list shows the reader all the books/other sources you've cited (or quoted) in your essay (I'll explain what citing is in a minute). A bibliography uses the same format to give the reader a list of books that *might also interest them* or provide *more information not directly related to your topic*, and that you have *not* used directly in your work.

You won't be expected to provide bibliographies for much undergraduate work; perhaps at the end of a longer assignment, like a dissertation. However, you'll always have to provide a reference list.

Here's an example:

You're writing a dissertation about the subtext of modern Japanese horror films. You've read, as part of the whole course, a 30-year-old book that is seen as key reading in the field. It discusses ways in which to analyse films *in general.* You haven't quoted it in your essay. However, you think that interested readers will benefit from reading it, and gain more from your dissertation by reading it. So you put it in your bibliography.

If you *have* used the book, by writing a sentence like, 'The basis for my analysis can be found in…', then it belongs in your reference list.

So what is citing? 'Citing' (the verb) or providing a 'citation' (the noun) is pointing out to the reader where, exactly, in your assignment you're referring to a particular source. If you quote a book, you provide a citation in that particular sentence so the reader can see straight away that the quote has come from somewhere else. If you quote the same book in your next paragraph, you have to provide a citation there as well. If you provide a chart or diagram, from a different book, on the next page it too comes with a citation. Think of 'citations' (which vary depending on your referencing system) as the bits of information you attach to quotes – although, as you'll see, it gets *slightly* more complicated than that.

Then the reader can use the citations to look at the *full references*, in the reference list – usually at the end of the essay. Some referencing systems, like footnoting, provide full references at the bottom of each page.

This is where you provide a lot more information about your sources – usually details like the publisher, all the authors' names, editors, and so on; this is the information your reader would need to go and find a copy of that same source.

There is a simple reason these two things are done separately. Imagine including all the information I've mentioned in the previous paragraph every time you quote a book, within the sentences of your essay! It would severely disrupt the flow of your writing and make your work very difficult to read. Citations are like quick 'keys' that point the reader to the full reference.

Citing and referencing are both necessary to provide your readers with enough information. There are also two different types of citation you can use – this refers mainly to written text, rather than images or multimedia.

You can *quote* other authors (also known as citing them *directly*) or *paraphrase* them (citing them *indirectly*).

Quoting is using someone else's *exact words*. If you take part of someone else's sentence and use those same words in the same order as the original text, that is quoting, and citing directly. If you use someone else's whole sentence, that is the same thing. If you take a whole paragraph from another text (which should happen only very rarely) and use it in an appendix you've written you are *quoting* someone else's work, and citing them directly. These are all direct citations.

Paraphrasing or citing *indirectly* means using *your own words* to express ideas that have come from another source. Paraphrasing might also mean using your own words to describe a diagram or visual element from something you've read. Think about it – you are still using *your words* and your own writing to engage with someone else's ideas.

The different referencing systems/styles

Referencing 'systems' and referencing 'styles' are the same thing. A system or style is the actual *type* of referencing you'll use, which dictates what your references look like, how they are inserted into your text, and how you construct a full reference list.

I can't tell you which system you'll be using at university. It depends on the subject you're studying; whether your university has a preferred system/style; whether your department has a preferred style; and sometimes on what your tutors themselves prefer or expect. Sometimes, your tutor won't specify a particular style, as long as you use a recognised system and do so correctly.

Each system will have a different format for direct citations, indirect citations and full/long references.

Most of the journals and books you'll read will have reference lists and referenced sources. Remember that your lecturers have to follow the same rules you do when they publish books or articles! Don't worry if the sources you read reference things differently – journals, for example, quite often have their own referencing systems, unique to them. The same thing applies to some publishers.

> **Key Point**
>
> In this book, my examples use the Harvard referencing style.

I can give you some examples of the more common systems used at universities in the UK, but be sure to check with your department, course handbook and tutors.

In the 'further reading' list at the end of this chapter, you'll see a book called *Cite Them Right*. This book contains many detailed examples of different kinds of source in the different referencing styles. For more detail on the different systems, I'd highly recommend this text.

These are the most common systems, and I've given some examples of the subjects that most commonly employ them (there are exceptions, however. Some universities in the UK, for example, recommend the Harvard system to all their students):

- Harvard referencing/the author–date system (widely used across a range of subjects)
- Vancouver/numeric referencing (Engineering, Design)
- Footnotes (English, History)
- MLA referencing (also used for Humanities)
- APA (Psychology; very similar to Harvard style)
- OSCOLA (Law)

These systems all involve citing (directly and indirectly) and providing full references, but they do so in different ways. I will give a quick summary of each, as well as an example citation and full reference.

Key Point

It is *crucial* you double-check what is expected of you. I've made this point several times, and it is very important! You might even find that one of your module tutors doesn't mind which system you use – that doesn't mean you can make one up! Also, do *not* try and 'memorise' how to cite and reference in a particular style. Your university will provide guides and webpages on referencing, and there are plenty of good books out there that explain how to reference any source – from a photocopy of an old manuscript that has been used in a lecture, to a blog post on the Internet, to a simple book, to a poem in an anthology.

Your lecturers, even the most experienced ones, will sometimes have to remind themselves how to reference a certain type of source, and look up an example. I know I do! The more you write, the more you reference, the more quickly it comes naturally. Of course, even though it eventually comes naturally, you still need to carefully check and double-check your reference lists as part of your proofreading process, to find small mistakes that might lose you marks.

Remember that these are intended to be *basic* summaries.

Harvard referencing/the author–date system

The Harvard system is based on putting citation information in brackets as part of your sentences.

> **Key Point**
>
> Harvard referencing is a commonly used system at many British universities. However, although the basic principles of the Harvard style remain the same, Harvard referencing in practice can differ slightly from book to book, or institution to institution. The examples here might not be identical to examples you're given by your tutors. Remember – they're marking your work, so provide the references they ask for!

This is usually the authors' surnames (unless you've used them as part of your sentence), the year of publication and a page number if you are citing directly. The full reference then also provides the place of publication, the publisher and the edition of the book, if necessary. The reference list is arranged alphabetically at the end of the essay.

> ✓ Example citation: One recent critic went as far as calling the film's dialogue 'unnecessarily inflammatory' (Davies, 2007, p36).
>
> ✓ Full reference: Davies, A. (2007) 'Fury and free speech: drawing the line', in Gordon, J. (ed.) *Contemporary Cinema and Relative Realism*. Oxford: Oxford University Press.

In the box below are two more sentences from a text discussing the education policy of John Major's government. Both include in-text citations in the Harvard style.

> ✓ Under his 'Citizen's Charter' he determined to institute a fully independent inspectorate so that eventually organisations would be able to tender for contracts to inspect schools (Major, 1999).
>
> ✓ The Education (Schools) Bill which enabled this system came to Parliament as a result of an internal review of the inspectorate carried out at the behest of Kenneth Clarke, but his plans to allow school governors to choose and then buy in particular inspection teams were thrown out by the House of Lords just prior to the election of 1992 (Balen, 1994).

Here is an excerpt from a Harvard list of full references, with a variety of texts included, ordered alphabetically by the surname of the authors:

References

✓ Abell, J & Walton, C (2010) Imagine: towards an integrated and applied social psychology. *British Journal of Social Psychology, 49,* 685–690.

✓ Abelson, R P (1995) *Statistics as principled argument.* Mahwah, NJ: Erlbaum.

✓ Abraham, C & Hampson, S E (1996) A social cognition approach to health psychology: philosophical and methodological issues. *Psychology and Health, 11,* 223–241.

✓ Adams, E W (1966) On the nature and purpose of measurement. *Synthese, 16,* 125–129.

✓ Afkhami, R, Higgins, V & de Kort, S (2009) Ethnicity: Introductory User Guide. Economic and Social Data Service Government. Retrieved from http://www.esds.ac.uk/government/docs/ethnicityintro.pdf (accessed 02/12/2012).

Vancouver or numeric referencing

In this system, you assign each of your sources a number, and simply put the number in brackets as part of the sentence you use them in. You then organise a full reference list, in the order of these numbers, at the end of the work. If you quote a particular book, which is source number '2', several times during your essay, just repeat the same number appropriately. Your reader can then check your reference list to find more information about source '2'.

✓ Example citation: One recent critic went as far as calling the film's dialogue 'unnecessarily inflammatory' (3).

✓ Full reference: Davies, A (2005) Fury and free speech: drawing the line. In Gordon J, ed. *Contemporary cinema and relative realism.* Oxford: Oxford University Press, pp. 30–45.

Footnotes

Footnotes are found across a range of subjects but tend to be more common in the Humanities, and in particular English. If you cite a source in a sentence, you put a small superscript number (like this[1]) that points the reader to the

---

[1]Your full reference goes here.

bottom of the page, where they will find more information about your source (take a look at the bottom of this page). There are various rules and techniques around using the same source twice, and even some Latin abbreviations you might get to grips with.

There is a similar style called 'endnotes', where the small numbers are used, but the full references are provided in a list at the end of a chapter or essay.

The following is a passage of text from a footnoted work. You'll see the numbered citations in the text itself, and the footnotes at the bottom of the page.

> ✓ … other Hittite texts, the strange deathbed text of Hattusilis I, in which the dying king, who had already rejected his own sons, now rejects his once favourite nephew as his royal successor and tries to settle the succession on his young grandson[2]; and the edict of Telepinus, in which Telepinus attempts to regulate the accession so that the bloodshed of royal assassinations and usurpations that had marred the most recent history of the Hittite throne could be avoided[3]. This despite the fact that Telepinus himself became king only by driving out king Huzziyas and his five brothers. It is not entirely clear why some usurpers of the throne felt this need for self-justification while others did not. Neither Tiglath-Pileser III nor Sargon II, two famous Assyrian usurpers, provide a defense of their accession analogous to that of Esarhaddon, though it should be noted that the damaged annals of both kings are missing the introductory section[4]. However, it may be that the pressure to provide such a defense was much greater when the new king was faced with ongoing opposition, hostility, and even rebellion after his initial success in seizing the throne. This was certainly the case with David, when the revolt, first of his son Absalom, then of the Benjaminite Sheba, revealed the ongoing ambivalence of the northern tribes toward David. It is worth noting that Sheba was from the same tribe as Saul, David's predecessor, and that Shimei, another Benjaminite from Saul's own family, publicly castigated David as a murderer and interpreted Absalom's revolt as God's judgment against David for David's bloodshed in overthrowing the dynasty of Saul (2 Sam 16: 5–8).

---

[2]F. Sommer and A. Falkenstein, Die hethitisch-akkadische Bilingue des Hattusili I (Labarna II) (Abh. der philosophisch-historischen Abteilung NF, 16; Munich, 1938).

[3]Sturtevant and Bechtel, A Hittite Chrestomathy, 175–200.

[4]For Tiglath-Pileser III see H. Tadmor, The Inscriptions of Tiglath-pileser III King of Assyria (Jerusalem: Israel Academy of Sciences and Humanities, 1994); for Sargon II, see A. Fuchs, Die Inschriften Sargons II. aus Khorsabad (Göttingen: Cuvillier, 1994).

Modern Language Association (MLA) and American Psychological Association (APA) referencing

MLA and APA referencing are very similar to Harvard referencing. I won't confuse you by giving you more examples here. Refer to your tutors and course handbooks if you're instructed to use MLA.

OSCOLA

OSCOLA stands for 'Oxford Standard for the Citation of Legal Authorities'. It is a system used almost exclusively in Law. Other referencing systems have ways of referencing legal material. You might, for example, be a social sciences student writing an essay about free speech. You might have plenty of laws to use and discuss in your work.

Law students, as you'd expect, make the *most* use of legal materials! OSCOLA can be quite a complex system. A lot of it is linked to knowledge of the subject, and what type of law you are discussing, or what journal a quotation has come from. You should be given guidance if you're expected to use this referencing style. Use the examples you're provided with!

✓ For the in-text references, OSCOLA uses footnotes. The formatting of full OSCOLA references depends on the type of legal source used. References to bills, statutory instruments and laws passed after 1963 (to name just a few types) will look different. Additionally, certain commonly-used law reports are identified by unique abbreviations.

✓ This might sound like a lot to take in. As always, though, the important thing for law students is to understand why referencing is important. Use whatever guides and resources are available to help you, and don't focus on memorising every single rule!

The 'p' word: plagiarism

You're likely to hear the word 'plagiarism', and the importance of making sure you don't plagiarise, mentioned a lot by your tutors at university. You'll probably hear a lot about it during the early weeks of each term, or academic year.

The good news is, if you learn how to reference correctly and ensure you do so every time you write an assignment, you are almost guaranteeing the absence of plagiarism in your work. Let's take a quick look at what plagiarism is and how we avoid it.

Plagiarism can be defined in various ways, but most universities have very similar definitions. To keep things simple, I'll use the definition from the Senate Regulations where I work:

> 'Plagiarism is the knowing or reckless presentation of another person's thoughts, writings, inventions, as one's own.' (Brunel University, 2012)

An important part of that definition is the word 'reckless', which means 'without knowing'. *Not knowing* that you must not plagiarise (so not knowing that you need to reference), or *not knowing* you've plagiarised is *no excuse*.

So, you have to understand what plagiarism is and be vigilant when writing your assignments.

Remember that this is a very important issue for your lecturers and tutors, too – being accused of plagiarism is a serious matter. If a published journal article or book is found to contain plagiarised material, it can damage reputations.

I don't think it's useful to see this as a big negative issue that you must avoid to ensure you're not punished – you should see *referencing* as a positive, necessary part of writing assignments. Work hard at getting *that* right, and you probably won't fall foul of the plagiarism rules at your university.

Critical thinking

There are plenty of excellent books for students that discuss critical thinking in more detail than I have space for here. The academic skills service at your university, or study skills tutors in your department, should be able to provide excellent advice.

Because it is vital to develop your critical thinking to succeed at university, and because it is a topic so linked with referencing, I will give you some key tips.

> **WHAT YOUR TUTORS SAY**
>
> 'When writing an academic piece of work, you should always use supporting references and, in particular, peer-reviewed journal articles. The use of a variety of sources within your work shows that you have read widely (i.e. beyond the lecture notes and recommended textbooks) and that you are able to identify key pieces of information.' – Kelly, Sports Psychology lecturer

Critical thinking can be defined in many ways. So, unfortunately, I can't give you a clear-cut definition. I can give you some ideas that will help you reach your own definition, however. Then you will develop your sense of what critical thinking is. Kelly points out the importance of identifying key ideas in what you read. This is an important part of critical thinking, to which I would add the following.

Critical thinking means:

- looking for the key ideas, themes and concepts in your research
- comparing, contrasting and linking the different ideas you identify
- understanding these ideas, and applying them to new questions or problems, rather than just memorising them
- contributing your own ideas to the academic debate; responding to the key ideas you've identified, not just summarising them for your reader. This is expected more and more of you as your progress through university

---

So how can you prove that you're thinking critically in your essays? Unfortunately, again, there is no easy answer, and developing your work at university often hinges on this point. It takes a while.

Here are some quick pointers:

- *Nearly every paragraph* you write should include at least one citation. There will be exceptions, but remember that you are being asked to *contribute* to the academic debate on your subject. If you don't bring that debate into your work by using other sources, you are just writing about your own ideas.
- On the other hand, don't construct whole paragraphs out of other references. Whenever you bring another source into your work, make sure it's clear to the reader why you've done so. Why is that reference important? Can you find another reference to reinforce it, or even contradict it, and then discuss these ideas together? Never insert a quotation and, in the hope that the quotation makes your point for you, just move on to a new paragraph or write your own sentence about something else. Even if the quotation is relevant, you are not being asked to find various relevant quotes and 'copy and paste' them into your own work.
- Don't just summarise: engage. Look at the difference between these two extracts from paragraphs using the same citation:

✗ Johnson (1998, p7) points out that 'children who are victims of bullying in primary school are more likely to be perceived as bullies by co-workers and friends in later life'. Bullying is a very important topic, because being a victim leads to the victim bullying others.

> ✓ Johnson (1998, p7) points out that 'children who are the victims of bullying in primary school are more likely to be perceived as bullies by co-workers and friends in later life'. Thus a kind of vicious circle is created, in which bullying leads to more bullying. This means tackling bullying during early years is important, an idea also raised by Davies and Jarman (2003).

The first brings in a quote, and then the writer of the essay uses a rather unimpressive word 'important' (remember, it's likely that most of the things you write about at university will be important!). Then the writer, essentially, repeats or summarises the quote in his/her own words.

The second uses the same quote, but engages with it and makes an argument – by suggesting that the quote provides evidence that tackling bullying at primary school will have later positive results. The writer has then brought in another indirect citation to reinforce his/her point.

Use a mixture of paraphrasing and direct quoting. Usually, it is better to paraphrase than quote directly, because it proves to the reader that you've understood an idea so well that you can express it in your own words. Sometimes, however, a well-chosen quote can illustrate your skill in knowing when someone else has written it best. It is better to have more indirect citation than direct. I tend to recommend that about two-thirds of your citations are indirect, and one third direct.

Introduce a mixture of different types of source. Books can contain lots of information, but can be slightly dated. Journal articles can respond to something much more recent, but tend to be more specific and complex. Show that you are comfortable with both. Additionally, avoid quoting extensively from introductions and early chapters in books. Your reader will see that you're only engaging with your reading at a basic level. The same goes for repeatedly referencing the same source throughout an essay. Your tutors want to see that you are really involved in a subject, not just one text.

Avoid quoting complete sentences. Direct quotes should always be worked into a sentence of your own. Three examples are set out below. In the first, I simply 'copy and paste' a whole quoted sentence into my paragraph:

> ✗ Attitudes to pre-emptive war, such a pertinent topic during modern times, particularly because of recent events in Iraq, and the nature of war reporting, have led to a shift in popular thinking about Western foreign intervention, particularly in the Middle East, that parallels popular thinking on display during the Vietnam War. 'By many measurable standards the years between 2000 and 2010 have been the most peaceful on record, though popular media leads many to think otherwise' (Richards, 2011, p47).

Here, I make some attempt to actually work part of the quote into my sentence:

> ✓ Attitudes to pre-emptive war, such a pertinent topic during modern times, particularly because of events in Iraq, and the nature of war reporting, have led to a shift in popular thinking about Western foreign intervention, particularly in the Middle East, that parallels popular thinking on display during the Vietnam War. However, according to 'many measurable standards the years between 2000 and 2010 have been the most peaceful on record, though popular media leads many to think otherwise' (Richards, 2011, p47).

Here, I make a full attempt to engage with the quote, by integrating it into my own sentence and making an argument:

> ✓ Richards highlights the effect that the 'popular media' and war reporting have had on attitudes to pre-emptive war, a pertinent topic during modern times particularly because of events in Iraq, causing popular thinking about Western intervention in the Middle East to parallel attitudes during the Vietnam War years despite the fact that according to 'many measurable standards the years between 2000 and 2010 have been the most peaceful on record' (Richards, 2011, p47).

In all examples, I cited – using the Harvard style – 'correctly'. However, in the first, I just dropped in a relevant quote, a complete sentence, that I hoped would do the work for me. This should *never* be done in your essays, and you'll notice that in the reading you do, it doesn't happen. No complete sentence that isn't written by you should stand alone in the middle (or beginning, or end!) of a paragraph of your own.

The second example is better, because the signposting language 'however' makes it clear that I'm making a contrast between the popular attitudes to war and some of the evidence suggesting that the situation is not as clear as it seems. I'm still using a long, complete sentence when quoting, however.

The third example is the best, because I have genuinely worked the original quote (in two parts, though that won't always be necessary) into my own paragraph, using the key parts of it *and* well-placed signposting language ('despite the fact that') to make the same point. Additionally, I use Richards' own phrase 'popular media' to save me repeating the idea of 'popular thinking' several times – it's only used once in the final paragraph.

Always make sure that quotes are worked into sentences *of your own*, even if they are complete sentences in themselves (like the second example) and where possible, craft your own sentence and use parts of the quote where it is appropriate (like the third example).

To give you some more ideas, I'll give you another final example of a similar paragraph, where I paraphrase Richards rather than quoting him directly:

> ✓ Popular attitudes to Western intervention, particularly in the Middle East, and the concept of pre-emptive war, have shifted substantially to resemble something like those on display during the later years of the Vietnam War. The impact of modern reporting, which is more instantaneous than it has been in the past, is, possibly, highlighted by the fact that some scholars suggest that in many ways, the past decade has been the most *peaceful* in history (Richards, 2011).

Here, I have very quickly summarised Richards' work and actually drawn a conclusion from it (that it might show the impact of differences in modern reporting). Because I've paraphrased, it is clear that I am engaging with the ideas. If I'd read several studies that reached the same conclusion that Richards did, I could quite quickly reinforce my point by citing them too. Here is an identical paragraph that uses referencing to reflect the fact that I have read *three* journal articles, books or studies that see the past decade as being our most peaceful:

> ✓ Popular attitudes to Western intervention, particularly in the Middle East, and the concept of pre-emptive war, have shifted substantially to resemble something like those on display during the later years of the Vietnam War. The impact of modern reporting, which is more instantaneous than it has been in the past, is, possibly, highlighted by the fact that some scholars suggest that in many ways, the past decade has been the most *peaceful* in history (Richards, 2011; Schofield, 2011; Philips & Markman, 2012).

In conclusion, there are many ways in which we can use referencing as a technique, and not just a 'box' we have to 'tick' to make sure we don't lose marks in an essay. Although referencing poorly *will* cause you to lose marks, as you become a more advanced writer, you'll become much better at thinking about *how* to bring other sources into your work, when to paraphrase and when to quote, and how to integrate points other people have made into your own paragraphs – and the actual technical part of referencing 'correctly' will come naturally.

As with many other topics discussed in this book, a good way of learning how to reference effectively is to look at how it's done in what you read. The next time you are asked to read a journal article for a seminar, or take a book from your university library because it's on your 'recommended reading' list, take the time to look at how references are used by the authors. Like you, they *must* base their academic arguments on the research they've done. You'll see that the best writers, the published academics, follow the key tips I've suggested. You're likely to learn a lot more too, and absorb their ideas.

More complex referencing techniques

There are various techniques we can use in most referencing systems that allow you to be quite clever with your sources, and how you bring in your research. Even if you don't use these during your early essays, you might find them useful later on. It is quite likely you'll see these in your *reading* as well, so it makes sense to develop some familiarity with them.

The two I will focus on here are: the use of 'ellipsis' and the use of square brackets.

Ellipsis

Ellipsis means, quite simply, inserting three full stops (...) whenever you omit (leave out) words, phrases or sentences from your direct quotes. This can be useful in two ways. First, you can make your work more concise by eliminating small words that aren't necessary to understand the full meaning of the original quote. Second, if a long quote contains information that isn't relevant or necessary to make your point, you can remove the unnecessary parts. This, again, is an opportunity to make sure you are focusing on the topic or question at hand.

Here's an example. Let's say you are writing an essay about the importance of technology in teaching and learning. You find this sentence in a book about the history of the Internet:

> It is difficult to quantify the impact that the rise of the Internet has had on the manufacturing industry, on business, on entertainment, on education, on developing employees at work, and on politics, among many others.

Because your essay is about technology and *teaching and learning*, you can make your quote more concise by writing:

> Walters writes that 'it is difficult to quantify the impact that the rise of the Internet has had … on education' (2008, p209), and although this is true, this essay attempts to illustrate some positive benefits of this impact.

In this example, I've used ellipsis to pull out only what is relevant. This is an example of thinking critically; selecting only the key ideas and facts needed to make your point and answer your essay question.

I can also use this example to highlight how using the correct parts of a quote is a skill to be mastered.

If you were writing, for example, a dissertation that focused on the *problems* posed by assuming that the Internet and other technologies are all-powerful, and you wanted to make the point that it is a difficult area to research, you might simply use the beginning of the sentence, and write:

> Walters writes that 'it is difficult to quantify the impact that the rise of the Internet has had…' (2008, p209).

Square brackets

You can use square brackets to *add your own words* to direct quotes. This can serve various purposes, and you must be sure that you are *not adding anything that substantially changes the original meaning*. So there is an element of judgement here, and this punctuation must be used carefully.

Here are some examples of the different ways in which square brackets might be used. Note that sometimes they are used in conjunction with ellipsis.

Errors in the original

> ✓ Rivers discusses some examples of asking primary school children about their feelings around bullying. I used similar interview questions in my classroom. When asked about his experiences of bullying, one child said, 'the bullies was [sic] picking on me every day'.

Here, the '*sic*' means that the original quote contained something 'incorrect' (in this case, grammar). Because I've added the word to the quote, I have to enclose it in square brackets to show that I've done so.

Emphasis mine and emphasis in original

> ✓ The problem inherent in Walter's investigation into bullying (1997) is that it only discusses two schools, even though he still sees fit to draw the conclusion that 'bullying among schoolchildren is a damaging *and widespread* phenomenon' [emphasis mine].

In the above example, I have italicised a part of the sentence to draw attention to it. As long as I point out that this emphasis is mine, as the square brackets indicate, this is acceptable. If the original quote has italics, you can insert [emphasis in original] to make sure your reader is aware that you haven't changed anything about the source material.

Summing up

In conclusion, here are the key ideas to take away from this chapter:

Accept the fact that you will need to reference throughout your work. You'll need to reference consistently, use a mixture of direct and indirect quotes, and always juxtapose your references with your own conclusions and points. Use a range of different types of source and engage with them in different ways.

Your tutors can see straight away if you've been lazy with, or rushed, your referencing – particularly if your referencing is inconsistent and changes throughout an assignment. This happens far too much, and you will lose marks because of it.

When I teach, I sum up these points by saying:

> Critical thinking means that you are getting involved in the academic debate.

I'll give you a very simple example:

Let's suppose I have been asked to write an essay on America's decision to go to war in Iraq in 2003. Remember the difference between an academic essay and a chat between friends. If I were talking to my friends about this, emotions might run high, and I might use my own feelings to explain my *opinions* on this decision.

However, if I am to write an essay on the topic, and remain subjective, I need to research the topic. I need to read the views of academics, of journalists, of historians. I need to find statistics. As I am doing so, I will form an argument in which I will bring up all these ideas and present the reader with a conclusion.

I might still say that the decision was wrong, or right, but I will be doing so in a neutral way, presenting evidence that supports my argument. A more advanced essay would also raise evidence that *contradicted* my argument, and I would take care to explain that I was aware of this evidence, but it did not affect the conclusion I reached – and *why*.

Because I need to follow the same referencing rules you do, here is my full reference for the definition of plagiarism I quoted:

Brunel University (2012) 'Academic appeals and disciplinary matters', *Senate Regulations* [online]. Available at: http://www.brunel.ac.uk/about/administration/university-rules-and-regulations/senate-regulations/academic-appeals-and-disciplinary-matters (accessed 13/08/2012).

Further reading

Most of the books below discuss the relationship between critical thinking and using sources in essays. The more technical side of various referencing styles is discussed in *Cite Them Right*, detailed below.

Colin, N (2007) *The Complete Guide to Referencing and Avoiding Plagiarism*. Maidenhead: Open University Press.
Cottrell, S (2011) *Critical Thinking Skills: Developing analysis and argument*, 2nd edn. Basingstoke: Palgrave.
Deane, M (2011) *Critical Thinking and Analysis*. Harlow: Longman.
Godfrey, J (2009) *How to Use Your Reading in Your Essays*. Basingstoke: Palgrave.
Pears, R (2010) *Cite Them Right*, 8th edn. Basingstoke: Palgrave.
Williams, K (2009) *Getting Critical*. Basingstoke: Palgrave.

6

Conciseness and Clarity

At university, you'll be expected to read and write about complex ideas. You'll research the different conclusions of other writers, academics and experts. You'll learn about disagreements over certain topics.

The texts you read will highlight different research results. Across your reading, research will be interpreted differently. Different people will interpret the same texts differently. This is all part of the debate and discussion on particular subjects in the 'academic arena'. I use the phrase 'academic arena' to cover all the conferences, books, journal articles, presentations, seminars, and more that go with an academic topic. As a student, you are now a part of this academic arena, and are expected to involve yourself in these discussions.

It is best to discuss complex ideas as simply as you can. Academic texts might sometimes be difficult to read. This should, though, only be because of the complexity of the ideas in the texts – *not the writing itself*. Academic writing should be *simple*, easy to read and 'to the point' (that is, not include any irrelevant sections).

How do you achieve this, then? Unfortunately, I can't answer that question in one sentence, and I will struggle to do it in a whole chapter. In fact, I could write a whole book on this topic.

This is one of this book's more 'advanced' chapters. I recommend you make yourself as comfortable as possible with the key ideas in the previous chapters before tackling this one.

My aim in this chapter, rather than struggling through complex definitions of the words 'conciseness' and 'clarity', is to give you my own basic definitions. Then I'll provide a series of tips and techniques, with examples, that you can apply to your work. By understanding the examples, you'll build up a *practical* idea of how to make your assignments clear and concise.

Conciseness and clarity are two different ideas, but they are closely linked. Think of them as different but *related*.

Here are my definitions. If you get a moment, try and find some others; look in dictionaries; or, at the end of a seminar, ask your tutor what he or she thinks.

Conciseness means using as few words as possible to make your point *effectively*.

I include the word 'effectively' because conciseness is not *just* about stripping your writing down as much as possible. As you've seen, for example, using signposting language often enhances the way an essay flows.

Signposting phrases add to your word count, but can make your work more effective. Conciseness, then, means stripping your writing down while ensuring it stays effective and readable.

Key Point

A student once showed me an essay he'd had marked. The feedback suggested he should learn to make his points more 'succinctly'. Succinctness and conciseness are the same thing; both are quite commonly used in feedback, so I thought I'd point this out.

Clarity means doing your best to make sure that your readers have the best possible chance to understand your points.

Another way of saying this might be: clarity means leaving – again, to the best of your ability – no room for doubt or confusion in your readers as to what you are arguing or suggesting.

Key Point

Another word you might see in essay feedback is 'coherent'. 'Coherent' means clear; 'coherence' is the noun, like 'clarity', and finally, if work is described as 'incoherent', as you might suspect, it means the writing is unclear.

Look how clearly Emily makes her excellent point, below.

> **WHAT YOUR TUTORS SAY**
>
> 'Clear writing is clear thinking.' – Emily, Academic Skills tutor

By *writing* clearly and concisely, you're demonstrating to your audience that you are *thinking* clearly about your topic. This suggests that you have a firm grasp of your ideas; that you've engaged with relevant sources; that you are confident and comfortable discussing the topic; and that you are eager to take part in the academic debate.

Creating this impression for the tutor marking your work is, clearly, a worthwhile thing to do.

Key Point

If clear writing demonstrates your confidence with a topic, is the opposite true? Does writing that is difficult to understand mean that the writer is not confident?

Not necessarily. As you take your notes and turn them into essay drafts, then edit and proofread, you'll do your best to turn potentially unclear writing into clear work. That's what this chapter is all about.

However – let's say you've written a very complex paragraph. It's extremely difficult to read. You have some idea of what you're trying to say, and you keep trying to tidy it up, but you realise you can't. In this case, there's a good chance you've identified a particular point you are *not* confident making.

By recognising this, you can ask yourself *why* you're not confident making this point. There are many possibilities, but recognising that a problem exists is the vital first step.

Perhaps you haven't properly grasped the journal article you're referencing? Perhaps you're drawing the wrong conclusion from the evidence? Maybe you've included some text that isn't really relevant and can be removed? You might even have included a point just to come closer to a word count, and genuinely not have confidence in the point you've written.

Recognising the link between clear writing and clear thinking, as Emily puts it, is a very important thing to do.

Watch those word counts

With several essays to write and deadlines looming, it is very easy to fail to pay attention to an assignment's word limit. It's also easy to forget about your word count as you write.

Does this sound like a situation you've been in?

Essay word limits exist for several reasons. One reason is that your tutors don't want to go insane marking epic essays! However, your tutors also want to see how good you are at making a clear argument, and clear points, in a limited space. When *they* write for journals, or have books published, they have limits they have to stick to. My publisher gave me a word limit for this book when they agreed to publish it.

If you end up writing reports or documents during employment, you'll also find yourself working with limits. These skills will stay with you beyond university.

Word limits are an opportunity to learn how to express only the points that are necessary. This takes time, and it is difficult. I hope this chapter points you in the right direction.

Under a variety of subheadings, I'll give you some tips, hints and techniques to make your work clearer and more concise (in some cases, both). They aren't in a particular order. At the end of the chapter, I'll show you some example paragraphs and essay extracts and apply some of the techniques. You'll see how simple changes can make a big difference to your writing.

The examples below will give you some specific guidance, but there is much more *you* can do. The more you write, and the more you read, the better you'll get at writing clearly and concisely in a natural way, and not thinking about it so much.

Once you find yourself in this state of mind, and these things are happening naturally, you'll know your writing really is improving.

Redundant phrases

Below is a group of common phrases that can easily be replaced by *one* word. The phrases vary in length; in some cases you'll only be trimming the word count by one. However, because these don't affect the meaning of your writing – and might even enhance it – I recommend making these replacements. As usual, use your word processor's 'find' tool to track these phrases down.

At this moment in time = now

In order to = to

Because of the fact that = because

(Continued)

(Continued)

In this particular place = here

A lot of = many

Take into consideration = consider

First of all = first/firstly

Prior to = before

In the event that = if

Due to the fact that = because

A number of = several

A variety of = several

In addition to = additionally

There are other examples, of course. Sometimes you might choose *not* to cut these phrases, and others like them, automatically. You should demonstrate variety in your writing. You should not, however, *deliberately* use these phrases *instead of* the shorter options just to make your work seem more 'academic' or more 'formal'.

Key Point

Remember: your work will read academically if you use an appropriate written style, conform to the basic conventions discussed earlier in the book, and engage with a particular subject at the right level. Trying to write in a *more* formal way is not the right approach.

Other redundant phrases

It's very tempting to try turning a simple, easy-to-read sentence into a complicated one, because you think it's what your tutors want. It isn't. Here are some examples of what are technically called 'tautologies'. A 'tautology' is the same idea expressed twice (or more) in different words; it can also mean adding unnecessary words to a statement that must already be true. (Take a look at the example 'red in colour', below, for an example of the latter definition.) Some aren't common in academic writing, but others are frequently seen in essays. This is only a short list – try and think of some others.

Three in number = three

Red in colour = red

True facts = facts

Long in duration = long

Very unique = unique

A short summary = a summary

A new innovation = an innovation

Unnecessary repetition can also occur in longer passages. Here is an example from a medical essay:

✗ The patient died of a fatal dose of morphine.

'Fatal' has a specific definition: something fatal causes death. If the patient has died, the dose of morphine *must* have been fatal. If the dose of morphine is fatal, it *must* have killed the patient. As such, two options might be:

✓ The patient was given a fatal dose of morphine.
✓ The patient died as a result of his morphine dose.

Here's another example, from a biographical essay about a painter:

✗ During his most prolific period as an artist, he hid from his friends his secret alcoholism.

Hiding something means keeping something secret. So the artist's alcoholism, in this example, *must* have been secret. This is another example of how precise you need to be in academic writing, to demonstrate your level of control over your points and meaning. Here are two better examples:

✓ During his most prolific period as an artist, he hid his alcoholism from his friends.

✓ During his most prolific period as an artist, he kept his alcoholism secret.

Here is one last example:

✗ In the latest comparable case, the suspect was found guilty and imprisoned in Hull Prison.

Here, the verb 'imprison' and the noun 'Hull Prison' say the same thing about what happened to the suspect. If the proper name of the prison (which is 'Hull Prison') isn't crucial, you could use:

✓ In the latest comparable case, the suspect was found guilty and imprisoned in Hull.

If including 'Hull Prison' is necessary, try this:

✓ In the latest comparable case, the suspect was found guilty and sent to Hull Prison.

I have two other reworked versions of this example. The first could be used if the actual place or name of the prison is not a crucial point. The second shows that the phrase 'found guilty' could be removed from any versions of this sentence, if you are comfortable assuming that your readers will make the link between being 'found guilty' and then sent to prison. Here they are:

✓ In the latest comparable case, the suspect was found guilty and imprisoned.

✓ In the latest comparable case, the suspect was imprisoned.

> **Key Point**
>
> The examples of sentences in this section are important, because they illustrate a point I made in the chapter about constructing sentences. Each word you use has a definition. Awareness of the specific definitions of words allows words to be chosen carefully and the meaning of your writing tightly controlled.
>
> In the example from the medical essay, the definition of 'fatal' means that no other words or phrases are needed that tell the reader the patient died; that's precisely what 'fatal' does.

Avoiding expletive constructions

'Expletive constructions' have nothing to do with swear words in your essays. (You must avoid swearing in your essays too, of course!)

Expletive constructions are sentences or phrases that begin 'there is' or 'there are'. You can usually remove them. You may have to make minor changes to make the remaining sentence grammatically correct.

Here's an example, in an assignment discussing primary education:

> ✗ There are many schools which have implemented a more flexible curriculum.

becomes

> ✓ Many schools have implemented a more flexible curriculum.

Both sentences mean *exactly the same thing*. The second sentence is three words shorter.

Here's another example. This essay discusses medicine and its relationship with the law:

> ✗ There is a growing part of the scientific community that is concerned about how insufficient attention is paid to genetic research legislation.

becomes

> ✓ A growing part of the scientific community is concerned about how insufficient attention is paid to genetic research legislation.

In both the examples above, 'there is' and 'there are' have been removed. Then the words 'which' and 'that' have also been taken out so the sentences make sense. However, you can't quite do the same thing with a sentence like this one:

> ✗ There is a risk of Siberian Tigers becoming extinct.

You *can* change the sentence, more substantially, however. Two possibilities are:

> ✓ Siberian Tigers are at risk of becoming extinct.

Or, changing the sentence even more:

> ✓ Extinction threatens Siberian Tigers.

Removing expletive constructions makes sentences more concise, but has another benefit. Removing them shifts the emphasis onto more important parts of your sentence. In the first two examples, the reader is immediately aware that the subjects of the sentence are 'many schools', or 'a growing part of the scientific community'. The subjects of your sentences are more important than the phrases 'there is' or 'there are'.

I've suggested two options for removing the expletive construction in the third example. Your decision will depend on where you want the *emphasis*. What do you want the reader to read *first?*

The first option makes 'Siberian Tigers' your subject and the first thing your reader 'sees'. In the second, the subject is 'extinction'. You can see now how these choices subtly but powerfully affect your writing and what your readers take from it.

Using simple words instead of complex ones

A varied vocabulary is important in academic writing. Depending on what you're studying, you'll have plenty of subject-specific terms to use, too. Usually, however, if you have the choice between a simple word or phrase, and a complex one, choose the simpler option. Of course, the simpler option must be academically appropriate (not slang, or colloquial language).

Here are two sentences. They describe a chemistry experiment. Which one is easier to read? Do they mean the same thing?

> ✗ The experiment was initialised at 7pm, subsequently halted half an hour later owing to complications, and re-initialised the next day.

> ✓ The experiment was started at 7pm, then stopped half an hour later because of problems, and begun again the next day.

The word 'complications' might be appropriate, but I chose to change it for the simpler 'problems' in the second version.

I also replaced 're-initialised' with 'begun' so as not to repeat 'started', but I could easily have done so and written 'started again' or 'restarted'. Again, this demonstrates that writing clearly and concisely comes down to choices; as your writing develops, you'll learn how to make these choices more quickly and effectively.

The phrase 'owing to', with its use of the verb 'to owe' seemed awkward to me. As such, I used the more common 'because of', which is much simpler.

Key Point

As we're on the topic of conciseness, I thought I'd mention something else about the examples above. I replaced the complex word 'subsequently' with the simpler 'then'. Do we need either, though? They're examples of signposting language, making sure in this case that the reader understands the sequence of events.

The fact that the reader *knows* the experiment was stopped 'half an hour later' means that this signposting isn't needed; it's already there. I'd argue that in the reworked example, the word 'then' could be removed.

Here's another pair. This assignment is discussing the development and staging of a play:

> ✗ In the director's annotated copy of the script, an alternative opening for the play is proposed. The eventual decision to proceed with the original opening was later clarified by the director, who decided that the interaction between the lead characters exemplified the continual exacerbation of tension in the play.

✓ In his notes, the director suggested a different beginning, which was never used. He later explained that, in the original opening, the increasing tension in the play was already established by the main characters.

In the first example, 'the director' is repeated, because there are so many words between both uses of the noun. Using the pronoun 'he' risks confusion, and might damage clarity. In the second version, I've removed this risk.

I removed the mention of the 'script' so I could also get rid of 'annotated'. You may disagree here – it depends whether or not the 'script' has been mentioned earlier in the essay.

Additionally, I've used the active voice instead of the passive: 'an alternative opening for the play is proposed' is passive; while my 'the director suggests a different beginning' is active. I also changed 'proposed' to 'suggested' and 'alternative' to 'different'.

The key point of the second sentence seems to be that the director explained his decision, and what that decision meant in terms of the play. I chose to write this in a simple sentence, and changed complex words like 'clarified', 'exacerbation' and 'exemplified'.

Some of the changes I've made in the sentences are minor and wouldn't achieve much on their own, but do make a difference overall. The temptation to write in an overly formal, complex way is a tough one to resist, especially as you start reading well-written, academic journal articles and books. Replacing just one complex word with a simple one is a good start.

Simple sentences

Favour simple sentences over hard-to-read ones. I've already suggested replacing complex words with simpler alternatives. You need simple sentences too.

I've already explained what a 'simple' sentence means in a grammatical sense: a sentence that expresses a complete idea with one subject, verb and object.

In this section, by 'simple' I just mean, broadly, 'easy-to-read'.

If your sentences are too long, split them into smaller ones. Avoid excessive use of commas or other punctuation to extend sentences.

Take a look at these two example sentences about global warming research:

✗ It makes sense, according to some current literature, to emphasise, and to reinforce, wherever possible, the decreased likelihood of attaining sufficient research funding for scientists and academics who challenge, or appear to be challenging, the consensus on global warming.

✓ Some current literature suggests it should be emphasised that scientists and academics who appear to challenge the consensus on global warming are less likely to get enough research funding.

Both sentences make the same point. Rather than splitting the first example into shorter sentences, I've focused on eliminating complex phrases and words.

I could discuss the various changes I've made in detail – but let's stick with the main ones. The first sentence contains 39 words, the second 29. I have found the key, strong verb ('emphasise') and removed a phrase that doesn't really add anything to the sentence – 'it makes sense, according to literature, to emphasise' by using the word 'suggests'.

'Attaining' has changed to 'get'. I also decided that 'appearing to challenge' and 'challenge' can actually be covered by 'appear to challenge'. I changed 'decreased likelihood' to 'less likely'.

I also decided to replace 'sufficient' with 'enough', although I don't think that 'sufficient' made the sentence terribly difficult to read.

Now take a look at two example *paragraphs*. One is made up of long sentences, with many clauses and commas, and the other uses much simpler ones. You can see that the confusing effect of complicated sentences is amplified if many of them are used.

✗ Although much is made of, and there has been extensive discussion in the literature about (Young, 1992; Wilson, 1997; Fredrickson & Parfitt, 2003), the alliance between the United Kingdom and the United States, especially when the leaders of both the countries in question are of a similar ideological persuasion, several examples and instances exist that make the suggestion that the situation is more complex than it might seem from these arguments. Some especially pertinent examples might be the Thatcher government's condemnation of Reagan's invasion of Grenada in the year 1983, and in addition, more recently, the friendship and alliance, which the media made much of, between President Bush and Prime Minister Tony Blair. In the latter case, a right-wing President and a centre-left Prime Minister were united and brought together by a similar view of foreign policy, which famously culminated in the invasion of Iraq by both countries in 2003.

✓ The alliance between the UK and the USA has been discussed extensively in the literature (Young, 1992; Wilson, 1997; Fredrickson & Parfitt, 2003). These sources also suggest that the alliance is stronger when the countries' leaders are similar ideologically. However, some examples suggest that the situation is more complex:

(Continued)

(Continued)

most importantly, the Thatcher government's condemnation of Reagan's invasion of Grenada in 1983. More recently, the right-wing President Bush and centre-left Prime Minister Tony Blair were united in their approach to foreign policy, demonstrated by their invasion of Iraq in 2003.

Clearly the second paragraph is shorter. More importantly, it is much easier to read. It has been broken down into shorter sentences, and I've applied some of the other techniques discussed in this chapter.

Key Point

Academic writing, like other kinds of writing, is made better by variety. Paragraph after paragraph of sentences of the same or similar length, written in a similar style, make for dull reading. However, as you are beginning to develop your writing skills, it is better to write simply than to go to the opposite extreme and write convoluted sentences. Variation in your sentences will come in time, naturally, as your writing develops.

Does this belong here?

Parts of this chapter deal with conciseness on a word-by-word basis: removing phrases, replacing words, tidying up sentences, and so on.

However, you also have to think about conciseness more broadly, and this is a trickier idea. I can't provide examples that are as clear-cut as the others. Some of the examples at the end of this chapter might help.

A useful question to bear in mind while writing is: 'Does this belong here?' The word 'this' refers to 'this sentence', 'this paragraph' or even 'this chapter', if you're writing a longer piece of work. Essentially, it refers to a portion of your writing.

This question works on many levels, in many ways. Think about all the reasons you might have, as you go through a page you've written, for deciding the answer is 'no'. Here are the most obvious examples:

- This doesn't answer the question
- I'm just repeating what another article has said (see my brief tips for critical thinking)
- The statistics or examples I'm providing aren't relevant
- I've already made this point; I don't need to make it again
- This writing is descriptive; it is stating facts instead of demonstrating critical thinking

> **Key Point**
>
> In Chapter 4, I described an exercise in which you, as the author, had to answer several questions about each paragraph. What I'm discussing here has the same essential aims, but is going a bit further to gauge the level of critical thinking you've demonstrated.

When I am going through an essay with the student, if I find a paragraph that seems overly complicated, doesn't make sense or is hard to read, I ask 'why are you telling me (the reader) this?'

Sometimes the student will struggle at first. Eventually, however, after some discussion, we find that the actual main point is much *simpler* and we can remove unnecessary paragraphs and sentences.

> **Key Point**
>
> The main idea here is to make sure you are always answering the question you have been asked; or discussing what the essay has told you to discuss.
>
> I often find a good way of making this point is to use an example from my own teaching.
>
> I was talking to a group of occupational therapy students who had been given an assignment, so their tutors had asked me to give a lecture on effective writing, with the particular assignment in mind.
>
> The essay asked students to read a case study (basically, a long description of a patient with a particular condition – for example, a woman who had cancer but had not told her employer) and to describe what they'd do with that patient – what treatment they'd recommend, and, based on their reading and learning, why they'd do so. It made no difference whether the patient was real or not; students were being asked to apply their knowledge to a particular problem or situation. It's likely you'll be asked to do something similar, regardless of the subject you're studying.
>
> I had read some first drafts of the essay and noticed a particular problem: students were eagerly demonstrating their research by, in the early parts of their essays, referencing lots of statistics about various kinds of cancer – including kinds of cancer that the patient did not have.
>
> During the lecture, I clarified with the students, 'You have been asked, pretty much, to imagine you were doing the real work of an occupational therapist: sitting down with the patient and outlining a treatment plan to them, along with your reasons for doing so'.
>
> This, of course, was true, and my audience nodded.
>
> I then said, 'Do you think that if you sat down with this woman and spent a long time discussing cancer statistics, including statistics about other types of cancer, and statistics
>
> *(Continued)*

(Continued)

about cancer in other countries, that this would help her? Would it help if you began summarising, in detail, all the journal articles you'd read about the cancer she has?'

This got a laugh, but I'd made my point. I'd seen lots of well-written, correctly referenced, informative paragraphs that *did not answer the question*. As a result, students risked losing marks by wasting their valuable word count. *Every paragraph* you write, *every sentence*, must go some way towards doing what the essay as a whole does.

Key Point

Asking questions like 'why are you telling the reader this?' and 'why are you saying it now?' can be a useful exercise when studying with friends. Sit down in a pair or group, and take it in turns to read a page of each other's work. If you find yourself wanting to ask one of these questions, or something similar, *stop and ask* out loud.

If your friend can answer quickly and easily, then there probably isn't a problem. If you're studying different subjects, for example, you might not have the same basic knowledge of a topic that other readers will. If your friend struggles to answer, then you've identified an area they need to work on.

Sometimes, your friend will eventually reach an answer, as you talk, and find that the explanation is much simpler than what they've written down. If so, they should make a note of their answer and then think about working it into the essay itself. Alternatively, they might realise they need to remove a sentence or paragraph, or move one, or make its relevance clearer.

This can be a very useful exercise. Of course, you can do this on your own too; try and get used to asking yourself these questions, as if you were someone reading the essay for the first time.

Meaningless modifiers: 'very'/'really'/'extremely'/'severely' (and so on)

Academic writing should be precise. By 'precise', I mean that the points you make should be *specific*. If you can't be precise, you should make it clear to the reader by 'hedging' (which I've discussed elsewhere – using verbs that prove you are not jumping to conclusions, or are being careful with your arguments).

While modifiers (describing words) like 'very', 'really', 'extremely', and others like them, might be useful in creative writing, or journalistic writing, they serve little purpose in academic writing.

This is not to say that you'll *never* use them in an essay. However, is there a difference between these two example sentences?

> Ronald Reagan won the 1980 Presidential election by a large margin of the popular vote.

and

> Ronald Reagan won the 1980 Presidential election by a very large margin of the popular vote.

I'd argue that there is no *useful* difference between them. The word 'very' can be removed without damaging your meaning. I could also argue that neither sentence provides more quantifiable, verifiable information than the following:

> Ronald Reagan won the 1980 Presidential election.

It all depends on the points you are trying to make. The next example *does* provide more information:

> Ronald Reagan won the 1980 Presidential election with 50.7% of the popular vote, compared with Jimmy Carter's 41% and John Anderson's 6.6%.

What if your essay is not focused on statistics, or you don't want to assume that your reader knows that Reagan's victory is a large one, compared with many American elections? Reagan's sizeable victory might be your main point. You might have to *add* some information:

> Ronald Reagan won the 1980 Presidential election with 50.7% of the popular vote, compared with Jimmy Carter's 41% and John Anderson's 6.6%; Reagan's victory was larger than many American election outcomes.

This rather long-winded example makes the point that if you are overusing words like 'very', 'really', 'extremely', or similar words, you might want to think about adding actual statistics or verifiable information from your research. Alternatively, make the importance of your point clear to the reader, as I have done by making the comparison in the last example. If you don't think doing these things is appropriate, then remove the words.

The future tense/unnecessary signposting

In a previous chapter, I discussed verbs, and verb tenses, which tell you *when* the action of the verb happened (past tense), happens (present tense) or will happen (future tense).

The future tense, as you'll know, is made using the verb 'will' (which comes from 'to be') and then an additional verb. It is often unnecessary in academic writing. I see the future tense used where the present tense would be fine.

Sometimes use of the future tense also highlights a deeper problem – when the author of an essay is telling their reader what they *will* do in their work, instead of simply doing it *right away*. You are putting something off for no reason – and wasting your words.

Use your 'find' tool, as always, to search for the word 'will'. Take a look at this example:

> ✗ This essay will attempt to outline the stages of hand transplantation surgery. The first stage of this kind of surgery, like any other, is made up of sterilisation and preparatory procedures.

The first sentence is not needed. The author is providing a kind of 'mini' introduction to the topic raised in the very next sentence. If you write clearly, your reader will know what you are discussing. You could call this 'unnecessary' signposting. Instead of showing the reader where your writing is going, you are telling them something they already know.

First, remove that sentence. Then make clear what kind of surgery is being discussed by putting the noun 'hand transplantation surgery' into the remaining sentence. This gives us:

> ✓ The first stage of hand transplantation surgery, like other kinds of surgery, is made up of sterilisation and preparatory procedures.

Much shorter, and much clearer. Here's another example:

> ✗ A definition of 'compassionate conservatism' will be required before going any further.

Here the present tense could be substituted appropriately:

> ✓ A definition of 'compassionate conservatism' is required before going any further.

When you find the word 'will' in your work, you'll find that in *almost* all cases, you can use the present tense instead. This makes your work simpler, more concise, and provides a sense of immediacy that adds strength to your writing.

In this case, however, there's a deeper issue. The author is, essentially, saying that a particular definition is necessary 'before going any further' – that is, it's necessary *now*. So why not provide the definition now?

A better version of this sentence would begin:

> ✓ 'Compassionate conservatism' can be defined as…

To sum up, the future tense should only be used when it is actually needed to show that an action (the verb) will occur in the future, and not to signpost points that will be made later in your work – unless this is necessary, perhaps in your introduction. In most cases, it can be replaced with the present tense. In some cases, you might find you can enhance your writing by reworking your sentence or paragraph a little more.

Avoiding repetition

Repetition can be a problem in several ways. It can be a broad issue, where a point is made several times over the course of an assignment unnecessarily. I've deliberately repeated key points in this book; this is one of a few examples of how *my* writing does not stick to all academic conventions (which is itself a point I've repeated).

The focus of this section is on the repetition that occurs on a smaller scale. By this, I mean the repetition of certain words (usually, but not always, nouns) or phrases within sentences and paragraphs. Repetition should only be removed when it is happening so much that it betrays a poor vocabulary and/ or lazy writing. Don't try and use each word only once in every paragraph – it might not be possible.

As a *general* rule, take the repeated noun, turn it into the subject of the sentence, and add the additional information. I do this in the following example:

> ✗ Technology is often seen as improving access to information (Willis, 2005). This increased availability of information, whenever users want or need it, does have negative aspects. The dangers of an information overload have recently been demonstrated more and more in these arenas, to name a few: the legal implications of information access; privacy and freedom of information; the information employers and employees might have access to.

'Information' is repeated many times here. I'm going to use it as the subject of my sentence, and begin with it, before adding the other points ('access' is repeated, too, but only once, and as such doesn't damage the paragraph as much):

> ✓ Information, access to which has been improved by technology (Willis, 2005), when easily available, can cause problems. These dangers, caused by an information overload, have recently been demonstrated more and more in several arenas: legal implications; privacy; and employer and employee access to information.

Here is another example:

> ✗ Many texts have highlighted the negative aspects of Imperialism, whether the focus was on distinct examples of Imperialism, and historical empires, or Imperialism as a concept. Different components of Imperialism, or topics associated with empire (in particular, colonialism), have also been criticized thoroughly and effectively for the past 40 years. More recently, however, a more nuanced view has become increasingly prevalent in the literature. This view accepts and discusses the positive outcomes and effects of Imperialism, as well as the negative ones.

In improving this paragraph, my aim is to reduce repetition of 'imperialism' and 'empire':

> ✓ Imperialism as a concept and in its specific historical forms, as well as components associated with it (colonialism, for example), has been criticized thoroughly and effectively in the literature, by many texts, for the past 40 years. More recently, however, empire has been discussed with a more nuanced view that accepts and discusses its positive outcomes, as well as the negative ones.

Again, in the second example, I have two sentences; the first uses 'Imperialism' as the subject, and the second 'empire'.

Key Point

If you've made your writing as clear as you can, and you find repetition in your work – try and remove the repetition if possible. I recommend it because doing so can often make your work more concise and easier to read. If you find that you can't remove the repetition without *damaging* clarity, or using strange uncommon words, then don't spend time struggling to do so. Remove repetition when it can be done easily, and when it enhances your writing. This will, I emphasise, be the case much of the time; but not *all* the time.

The active and passive voices

I discussed this on page 63; it is important to understand this in the context of constructing sentences. It also impacts on clarity and conciseness, so this is a recap of the main points.

Sentences can be written in either the 'active' or 'passive' voice.

Put simply:

- The active voice goes: Noun/subject – verb – noun/object
- The passive voice goes: Noun/object – *some form of the verb 'to be'* – verb – *by* – noun/subject

---

The passive voice 'flips' the subject and object. The word 'by' has slipped into the sentence, along with the verb 'to be' in some form. Immediately, you sense that the passive voice is more complicated than the active voice.

This example shows an active sentence and its passive equivalent with added words in bold.

Active: Several scientists conducted a study into psychosis.

Passive: A study into psychosis **was** conducted **by** several scientists.

The next sentence is more complex; the active or passive voice can still be 'buried' underneath additional modifying phrases and clauses (remember that 'modifying' means providing additional information):

Active: Many articles published in the 1970s take a post-modern approach to science, particularly when the Shelleyian conflict between science-centric and humanist approaches comes to the fore.

Passive: A post-modern approach to science is taken by many articles published in the 1970s, particularly when the Shelleyian conflict between science-centric and humanist approaches comes to the fore.

It should be quite obvious that the passive voice *is* more complicated and potentially confusing than the active voice. *As a general rule*, write sentences in the active voice (search for the word 'by' with your word processor; you will of course come across many perfectly acceptable uses of the word, but you will also identify examples of the passive voice).

However, there are two main exceptions to this rule, discussed in more detail on pages 68 and 69.

The passive voice can be used:

- to avoid the first person (remember, the first person includes the pronouns 'I', 'we', 'us', and so on)
- to put more emphasis on the object of the sentence, depending on your aims when writing.

Here's an example of how the passive voice can be used to remove the first person:

> ✗ We conducted the experiment at room temperature.

becomes

> ✓ The experiment was conducted at room temperature.

Key Point

Remember that sentences in the passive voice can *still* be written in the first person – so writing a passive sentence doesn't automatically mean you've removed the first person!

For example:

> ✗ Our group was assessed by our teachers based on our teamwork.

For reference, the active version of this sentence would be:

> ✓ Our teachers assessed our group based on our teamwork.

A third-person equivalent might simply be:

> ✓ Teachers assessed the group based on teamwork.

Sometimes you might want to emphasise the object of a sentence over the subject. I'll use one of the earlier examples:

Active: Many articles published in the 1970s take a post-modern approach to science, particularly when the Shelleyian conflict between science-centric and humanist approaches comes to the fore.

Passive: A post-modern approach to science is taken by many articles published in the 1970s, particularly when the Shelleyian conflict between science-centric and humanist approaches comes to the fore.

If my focus in the paragraph, and what I'm going on to discuss in more detail, are attitudes to science in the 1970s, and how they've changed, perhaps, over recent or previous decades, then the active voice seems appropriate. If, however, this part of my essay, or my essay as a whole, is about post-modernism in science, I might choose to use the passive voice.

As you edit your work, favour the active voice over the passive. If, however, you think, 'I really do need to focus on the object here', then use the passive. If this results in a horribly complicated sentence, try a complete rewrite that puts the emphasis where it needs to be.

Changing negatives to affirmatives

Some of the sections in this chapter highlight techniques that do not correct 'mistakes'. This is one of them – you will never be marked down for using a 'negative' phrase (there's a definition coming shortly!); but, applying some or all of these techniques to essays as a whole *will* make the assignment read more clearly.

A 'negative', in grammar, is a phrase that includes the word 'not' or 'no', to express a lack of something, or the absence of a quality. Sometimes, we can shorten these, and also write more powerful, 'punchy' phrases, by replacing them with an 'affirmative' – one word (in most cases) that means the same thing.

Here are some basic examples – remember, look for 'no' or 'not' using the 'find' tool, as I keep suggesting.

Not different = the same
Not the same = different
Not allow = prevent
Not notice = overlook
Not many = few
Not often = rarely
Not stop = continue
Not include = omit

The last example, 'omit', demonstrates that sometimes the negative uses less complex words than the positive you might replace it with – so you may choose not to do so. The point is not to struggle to find positives for each time you've used 'no' or 'not', but to use an affirmative when it's an easy option.

Removing excessive 'nominalisation'

This is another recommendation that you could ignore completely and never be marked 'incorrect' in an assignment. This is quite a simple way of making very complicated, hard-to-read paragraphs or sentences seem more active. I'm not using 'active' in the grammatical sense, as discussed earlier in this chapter, but in the broader sense. Following the advice below will make your writing *move* more, and give a greater sense of progressing through points.

Look at the following words:

Nomination

Inflation

Management

Information

Experimentation

Nominalisation (the title of this section is an example of itself!)

All the words above are *nouns* that come from *verbs*. Because academic writing tends to be quite complex and formal, nominalisations appear quite often. Nominalisation is also often found in business and report writing. Note that most of them end in 'ion' – this is the big give-away. Some end in 'ment' (management, accomplishment, entanglement), but these are less common.

I recommend that you turn nominalisations in your work into verbs – in my classes, I say 'pull the verbs out!' The above nouns, transformed into verbs, become:

To nominate

To inflate

To manage

To inform

To experiment

To nominalise

This might seem like a small issue. To demonstrate the effect excessive nominalisation can have, I've written two paragraphs. In the second, I've 'pulled the verbs out'.

> **Key Point**
>
> We've established that verbs are, literally, where the *action* happens. I recommended in an earlier chapter using *strong*, clear verbs. This is another example of the same principle, used in a slightly different way.

Compare:

> ✗ The management decided that the nomination of Professor Stanwell, and his collaboration, would help them gather information about current experimentation with the configuration of the machinery.

and

> ✓ Managers decided to nominate Professor Stanwell to help collaborate and research current experiments and to configure the machinery.

Even though both sentences are saying the same thing, the second is much shorter. I didn't change 'management' into a verb 'manage', because it wouldn't work. However, the someone who carries out the verb 'to manage' is a 'manager', and I decided that the sentence was better with 'managers' instead.

Additionally, changing 'information' to the verb 'inform' would mean I'd have to change the sentence a lot more. Instead, I asked myself: what single verb is appropriate in place of 'gather information'? I came up with 'research'.

Partly because the second example is shorter, and partly because of the stronger verbs, it seems much more *active*. The second example is much easier to read, but still academically appropriate.

Here is one more pair of examples:

> ✗ One of the company's major achievements is the initiation of the implementation of a more advanced authentication system across all their work-stations. An explanation is provided by the company's CEO (Maxwell, 2011) who saw this as a vital security enhancement.

✓ The company has achieved much by beginning to implement a more advanced authentication system across all work-stations. The company's CEO explains that he saw this as enhancing security in a vital way (Maxwell, 2011).

The second paragraph is still shorter, but there are some differences here. Instead of turning 'initiation' into 'initiate', I went for the simpler 'begin'. I saw the opportunity to use a simpler word, as I recommended earlier in this chapter.

I didn't change 'authentication' because here it is actually being used in the subject-specific context – computer and network security. Turning this into a verb would also force me to do an awful lot of work reshaping the sentence.

In the second sentence, I turned the noun 'explanation' into the verb 'explain'. This also allowed me to change the sentence from the passive voice ('an explanation is provided by the CEO') to the active ('the CEO explains that…'), which I've also discussed in this chapter. The final change ('enhancement' to 'enhancing') did force me to add words ('in a vital way'), but I concluded that it is still easier to read. You might disagree.

Excessive nominalisation is a very simple issue to track down if you're using a word processor to type an assignment. (Yes, I'm recommending the 'find' tool again!) Simply type 'ion' and, separately, 'ment' into the tool.

It will show you each time you've used these letters. In many cases, you'll very quickly and easily be able to change the noun to a verb – my two examples are, probably, a little exaggerated. If you're finding that making these changes *changes the nature of your sentence*, or is *taking too much time*, then just make sure the sentence makes sense and move on.

Key Point

In that sense, this issue is like some others in the chapter – using nominalisations is not 'wrong', but I recommend editing them when possible. Don't spend a huge amount of time doing this, though. As you develop as a writer, you'll get better at realising what you should take time over.

That said, students entering Higher Education sometimes have the idea that they should strive for a strange, extreme kind of formality in their writing. They try and twist the English language beyond all recognition because that's what they think is expected of them. This results in some very strange paragraphs, like the examples I've used in this nominalisation section.

Don't do this twisting! Instead, craft clear, simple, appropriate sentences and paragraphs.

Using the word 'this'

The word 'this' (in most cases, it is, in grammar terms, a 'determiner', but it can also be an adverb) is, as you'd expect, very common. In academic writing, it is very important to make sure your reader knows what 'this' is referring to whenever you use it. Sometimes this will be obvious, but sometimes it's worth putting in a little effort to *make* it obvious. The problem with 'this' is that it is often used quite lazily to jump to the next point or topic in a sequence. Look at this example, from the introduction to an occupational therapy essay:

> ✗ Evidence has been found that links between occupation and well-being have been studied, examined, and dealt with by philosophers and men of medicine going back to ancient times – in ancient Greek society, for example (Rosen, 2001). The reforms of hospital systems in Europe in the 18th century included well-documented ideas that are still vital in the field of occupational therapy today (Riel & Seben, 2007).
>
> This belies the sense among some American medical associations that this form of therapy is a new or novel approach, which has been discussed by occupational therapists worldwide (Riel & Seben, 2007; Wilfred, 2010).

The word 'this' is a bit lazy. What does it refer to? A specific fact in the preceding paragraph? A specific *noun* in the preceding paragraph? The whole *idea* of the first paragraph? Although there is nothing 'wrong' with the example, in a more advanced essay, the author would make it much clearer what 'this' means – and by doing this, create a much better link between the paragraphs. This principle can also apply within sentences.

Key Point

Look at the last sentence in the previous paragraph – instead of 'this can also apply within sentences', I have followed my own advice, and written 'this *principle* can also apply within sentences'.

When you find you've used the word 'this', ask yourself what you are referring to, and ask yourself whether you think the reader will read it the way you intended. If in doubt, actually point out what you are referring to. I've changed the example above to provide this clarity:

> ✓ Evidence has been found that links between occupation and well-being have been studied, examined, and dealt with by philosophers and men of medicine going back to ancient times – in ancient Greek society, for example (Rosen, 2001). The reforms of hospital systems in Europe in the 18th century included well-documented ideas that are still vital in the field of occupational therapy today (Riel & Seben, 2007).
>
> This evidence, and in particular the strength of occupational therapy's key ideas in Europe, belies the sense among some American medical associations that this form of therapy is a new or novel approach, which has been discussed by occupational therapists worldwide (Riel & Seben, 2007; Wilfred, 2010).

Use the 'find' tool, and double-check your use of the word 'this'. Sometimes you won't need to do anything, but sometimes making some slight changes will make for much more coherent, developed writing.

More examples

As I wrote at the start of this chapter, actually explaining conciseness and clarity is difficult.

I hope that the techniques I've discussed here, and the examples in particular, have demonstrated some of the kinds of choices you can make to improve your writing. Learning when and where to remove, replace or add words and phrases is a skill you will develop as your writing improves.

In this last section, I'll go through a series of examples (very similar to examples I've seen in actual essays) and explain my reasons for changing them. I have adapted the passages shown to make them more concise, as well as easier to read.

At first, this way of thinking will be easiest during the editing and proof-reading stages of your work. Eventually you'll learn to apply these approaches as you're writing. Not all of the changes I've made are the only options, or even the 'best' ones, but are just *my* ideas. You may come up with your own.

By explaining them, I'm hoping to make clear the thought processes you might go through as you try to write as concisely and clearly as you can.

Example one

> ✗ US politicians faced the problem in 1994 that the public did not trust or look up to politicians; the public thought politicians were untrustworthy and did not vote to keep them in power.

We've discussed repetition as a potential issue. This sentence repeats two words several times – 'politicians' and 'public', as well as an idea – the idea of untrustworthiness, which is mentioned twice in different ways. To change this, I've decided to use the word 'politicians' as the subject of the sentence, to only use 'the public' once, and to only mention the idea of trust once (which actually makes it more powerful). So my new version is:

> ✓ US politicians faced the problem in 1994 that the public did not trust or look up to them, and would not vote to keep members of congress in power.

Example two

> ✗ There are many issues to examine in the results of the study. The first issue, the most important of the issues, is the fact that the placebo achieved the same results as the drug. The second issue…

This extract again makes heavy use of repetition ('issue'), which makes it read very poorly. The writer is also introducing a list where it isn't needed – clever use of the words 'first', 'second', and so on, as well as the plural 'issues' will make it clear to the reader that there are several. In a way, first, second, and so on can act as signposting language – clarifying to the reader in what order something is happening.

Additionally, the writer has used the expletive construction 'there are', which as I've discussed above can often be removed. So I came up with:

> ✓ The first and most important issue presented by the study is the fact that the placebo achieved the same results as the drug. The second is that…

Example three

The following example is from an English essay discussing Martin Amis' novel *Money*:

> ✗ In *Money*, Martin Amis makes the protagonist a man named John Self. The protagonist's surname is Self. This surname alone suggests fascination with oneself.

154

Here we again have some repetition ('self' and 'protagonist'). (For English students – note that if you've already made it clear what text you are discussing, or the essay question does so, you don't need to repeat the name of the novel unnecessarily, or the name of the author – you can assume your audience will be familiar with both. I won't make these changes here, but bear this in mind.)

Unfortunately, the repetition here undoes the work done by the word 'alone', which makes the point stronger, more emphatic. Additionally, the reader knows that the character's name is 'John Self', and as such, using the word 'surname' again is not necessary either. Another point, for English students is that you can assume your readers will be familiar with the text, and as such will know what the characters' surname is. Your tutors won't set essays on books they don't know! We can trim this heavily:

> ✓ The surname alone of Martin Amis' protagonist in *Money* suggests fascination with oneself.

Example four

The next example comes from an essay about the ethical treatment of patients during social work and after operations:

> ✗ In order to outline the key ethical principles that health professionals should follow when working with clients and patients, it may be beneficial to look at why ethical principles are an important part of the health profession. Therefore, a brief look at the historical development of ethics in healthcare is incorporated.

This is a more complicated one. It should be obvious that this is quite a complicated paragraph. It also repeats several phrases ('ethical principles'; 'health profession/professional'). It also makes the mistake of 'over-signposting'; the last sentence tells the reader, 'my essay will be doing this', instead of just doing it. Additionally, the use of the word 'may' is worrying; if a certain topic belongs in your essay, you should be sure it will be beneficial! As pointed out previously, 'in order to' can be replaced with 'to'.

In reality, this paragraph says: 'To outline x, it might be important to look at why x is important, so this essay will look at the history of x'. I propose quite a major change – make this sentence more introductory in nature, and then get right into the detail:

> ✓ Ethical principles and their history are an important part of the health profession.

By using my revised version, the author is setting up the reader for the upcoming topics (ethical principles, and their history, in the context of professional healthcare) and essentially forcing themselves to begin discussing those topics right away. In this example, removing repetition and making the sentence simpler was less important than actually thinking about whether much of it was necessary at all.

Example five

The following example comes partway through a psychology essay about Cognitive Behavioural Therapy (referred to in the example as CBT).

> ✗ In addition to this point, CBT is a set of practical methods of solving people's mental health problems, rather than methods that involve spending a great deal of time to discover the grounds for their illnesses.

The phrase 'in addition to this point' can easily be replaced with 'additionally'. (The positive thing about the original phrase is that the word 'this' has been clarified by addition of the word 'point'). I think the next clause in the sentence can be shortened quite dramatically. The verb is 'solve', and I think that should be stronger, so I'm going to use that. What additional information is provided about the solving; what modifiers are used? The key modifier is 'practical'. We also need to retain the subject – 'mental health problems'. However, I'd argue that we don't need to specify the fact that 'people' have these problems, because I think we can assume readers will know this.
So far, that gives us a new beginning:

> ✓ Additionally + CBT + solving practically + mental health problems =
> ✓ Additionally, CBT solves mental health problems practically...

This leaves me with the final clause. First, I think that 'rather than' can be replaced by 'without', though this isn't crucial. I've already eliminated the noun 'methods' from the middle clause – I'll try it again in the final part. The main verbs here are 'spending', as in 'spending a great deal of time', and 'discover'. 'Involve' is a verb, but it doesn't seem as important as 'spending'. Remember my recommendation to use strong, powerful verbs whenever possible. I have to change the form of 'discover', but that isn't a problem.

I think that 'a great deal of time' can be replaced with 'excessive time'. This is more concise, but the word 'excessive' reinforces the point that methods other than CBT don't just take time, they take *too much* time.

Because I have shortened the sentence, I can probably get away with using the pronoun 'their' instead of using the noun 'illnesses' or repeating 'mental health problems'. Add these ideas to my newly crafted beginning, and we get:

> ✓ Additionally, CBT solves mental health problems practically, without spending excessive time discovering their causes.

I'm going to make one final change. Although 'discover' is one of the important verbs in the sentence, it creates a sense of almost 'accidental' discovery. I want a *stronger* verb that suggests methods other than CBT take excessive time looking into, seeking out or finding root causes or problems. How about 'investigate'? My final version:

> ✓ Additionally, CBT solves mental health problems practically, without spending excessive time investigating their causes.

Key Point

Some of the changes I made to the examples above were quite complex. I have quite a lot of experience helping students with essays, as well as writing my own, and doing plenty of other writing. As such, some of this comes quite naturally to me. Not all of it, however. It took me a while to decide to make my final change of 'discovering' to 'investigating'. You might not agree with that change, or have other ideas. The same goes for some of the other changes I've made.

What I've tried to do with these examples is demonstrate the thought process behind making work clearer and more concise. Try and think about your work in the same way; work in groups, and think about the work of your friends and peers in the same way.

Further reading

The books listed below discuss techniques and ideas that can help you develop as a writer. Some are not restricted to academic writing, but as you get more comfortable with writing assignments, you'll find these very useful. Because of the nature of these texts, I've provided you with some points to bear in mind for some of them.

O'Driscoll, J (1984) *Penguin Advanced Writing Skills*. London: Penguin.

Orwell, G (1946) 'Politics and the English Language' in *Shooting an Elephant and Other Essays*. London: Penguin Modern Classics.

George Orwell's comments on writing, and his ideas as to what makes writing good, are somewhat timeless. This essay in particular is essential reading for anyone developing their writing – even if you don't read the whole thing, which goes into detail about the relationship between politics and language, look for Orwell's six rules on writing. I've never read a better series of instructions to keep language clear and concise. The rest of the book is well worth a read if you are genuinely interested in writing as an art, and one of its greatest advocates.

Orwell, G (1946) Politics and the English Language [online]. Available at: http://www.orwell.ru/library/essays/politics/english/e_polit/ (accessed 27/08/2012).

This is a link to the essay mentioned above, available online. Start here, perhaps, but do investigate the whole book of essays.

Strunk, W & EB White (2000) *The Elements of Style*, 4th edn. Harlow: Pearson Longman.

Originally written in 1918, Strunk and White's short book contains clearly written advice on clarity and conciseness. The book has been well known since it was published, and although its reputation is not as good now as it used to be, it is still worth a read, as some of the advice is still crucial today.

Swales, J (2000) *English in Today's Research World: A writing guide*. Ann Arbor, MI: University of Michigan Press.

Zinsser, W (2006) *On Writing Well: The classic guide to writing non-fiction*, 7th edn. London: HarperCollins.

7

Common Mistakes and
How to Deal With Them

This chapter deals with a variety of issues and mistakes that I have seen many times in essays. Some readers might recognise many of the issues here. Others might notice only a few areas for improvement in their own work.

Some of these issues are actual *mistakes*; sentences that contain them are grammatically wrong. Others, however, are not 'mistakes' in the sense of being incorrect: they might damage your writing in some other way.

Some of the issues have complex origins, some much simpler; some are easy to track down, while others are tougher to spot.

This chapter also includes some 'quick tips'. These are smaller bits of advice, dealing with easy-to-solve issues.

As you read through this section, remember that these issues are problematic because they hinder your writing's clarity, simplicity and effectiveness; and, therefore, your meaning. By now, you should realise how important these qualities are.

It is important to have an idea of context. If you've made one of the more minor mistakes, just once, you might not be penalised. However, if they appear throughout your work, or your essay includes a range of recurring mistakes, you are damaging your chances of getting the best marks. The more substantial issues might affect your mark in themselves.

I've identified these issues based on the experience I have had, and my colleagues have had, reading many kinds of assignments from a wide range of subjects. View these pages not as a warning, but as an opportunity.

You have the chance to learn where you can improve your writing, by avoiding the more common issues that appear in essays. Avoiding these will allow you to focus on developing your writing as a whole.

As you read, start to think about the nature of your own writing. Think about how likely it is that the issues discussed here are appearing in your essays. You might recognise some of them immediately.

Note that some of the mistakes identified here have already been mentioned in the book. Even so, I wanted all these common issues to appear together, to give you an idea of the kinds of things to start looking for as you write.

Additionally, I think I should repeat here the fact that this book does not stick to all the conventions of academic writing that I recommend. This might occasionally be noticeable in this chapter.

Mixed constructions

A 'mixed construction' will be grammatically incorrect. *How* it is incorrect will depend on the sentence itself. However, mixed constructions of various types appear commonly in essays.

Mixed constructions are sentences that are made up of various parts that do not connect properly grammatically. The different parts of the sentence might be linked by the same topic, or they might *almost* link in a grammatical way – but the result is a sentence that is incorrect, at best; at worst, mixed constructions can be potentially confusing to a reader.

If you follow the subject–verb–object rules discussed earlier, and ensure your verbs and pronouns agree, and construct sentences carefully, you shouldn't have too much of a problem with mixed constructions.

Most commonly, a mixed construction is a sentence that begins by saying one thing, and then shifts into a different kind of sentence. Let's look at some examples:

- ✗ Local government has had a variety of responsibilities in the UK however a successful result for the main political parties.

- ✗ In this experiment, quantities of several corrosive chemicals that are needed.

- ✗ Although the play's two main characters seem to be redeemed, but the outlook can be considered bleak.

Read the sentences aloud; they certainly *sound* wrong, somehow, don't they? I will examine them in order.

- ✗ Local government has had a variety of responsibilities in the UK however a successful result for the main political parties.

Here, the subject–verb–object arrangement operates correctly up to 'in the UK'. After that, there's a problem. The word 'however' does not properly connect the second part of the sentence with the first, which is, really, just a modified noun ('successful result' with some additional information). A verb of some kind is missing. 'However' does not seem to be the right conjunction in any case. Additionally, though, the problem with meaning is deeper here. It's not quite clear what the writer is actually saying. Determining this would be the first step in rectifying the problem. I will rewrite the sentence as if the point is that British local governments always have a certain set of responsibilities, regardless of the party in power in Parliament:

> ✓ Local government has a variety of responsibilities, which exist regardless of which political party is in power.

> ✗ In this experiment, quantities of several corrosive chemicals that are needed.

This example is missing something; there is the sense that the sentence needs *more*. The reason for this is the word 'that' towards the end of the sentence. If the writer is simply pointing out the need for several corrosive chemicals, not much needs to be done: the sentence begins with a modifier, 'in this experiment'. A subject–verb agreement follows: the subject/noun is 'quantities of several corrosive chemicals'; the verb is 'are needed'. This is a rare sentence with no object. It is clear that the word 'that' performs no function. To solve this problem, I will remove 'that' and make the first part of the sentence the object:

> ✓ Quantities of several corrosive chemicals are needed in this experiment.

If the word 'that' appears because the writer wants to do *more* with the sentence, by suggesting perhaps that the need for corrosive chemicals leads to *something else*, then the sentence is more confusing. Again, the writer has to think through what they mean. Something like the following would be possible, of course:

> ✓ The quantities of corrosive chemicals that are needed in this experiment are substantial enough that specific certified laboratories can carry out this work.

Sometimes, as you can see, mixed constructions are mistakes that come from hurried writing. If you proofread carefully, you are likely to find them. Some of them, though, highlight a problem with unclear meaning. This, again, proves the importance of a common theme of this book – being sure of what you want to tell the reader.

The third, final example comes from a theatre studies essay.

> ✗ Although the play's two main characters seem to be redeemed, but the outlook can be considered bleak.

The problem here is that the word 'although' sets up the sentence's second half to provide a contradictory phrase – which it does – the word 'but' has also been used. Using the two conjunctions has made the sentence confusing and incorrect. Removing either one solves the problem:

> ✓ Although the play's two main characters seem to be redeemed, the outlook can be considered bleak.
>
> ✓ The play's two main characters seem to be redeemed, but the outlook can be considered bleak.

There are, potentially, subtle differences of emphasis in the two different options, but ultimately, both sentences say the same thing.

Key Point

Two of the three mixed constructions I've written are underlined in green by my word processor's spell-checking and grammar tool. The software can tell that the sentence is grammatically incorrect, but *it can't tell me why*. Additionally, the first mixed construction is not marked as incorrect at all. This highlights the limitations of technology; the next chapter will discuss this idea a little more.

Reading sentences aloud is a good way to find mixed constructions. They will sound wrong, even if you don't know why at first. In general, conjunctions and missing verbs are common causes of the problem. Think through what you want to say, and write it in a calm and unhurried way.

Dangling modifiers

As you become more confident in your writing, you'll naturally (and correctly) try to vary your sentence structure more. As you do so, of course, you need to take care to check your writing is still grammatically correct.

This is a common problem. It occurs in sentences that begin with a modifying phrase before the traditional subject–verb–object arrangement. Quite often these modifying phrases involve a verb ending in 'ing', or some other descriptive phrase made up of several words.

Here are two *correct* examples of this kind of sentence:

> ✓ Feeling pressurised by declining ratings, the executives changed the television network's advertising policy.
>
> ✓ Originally developed to enhance efficiency in local health authorities, the new database system played an important role in directly improving the experiences of service users.

These examples are correct, because the first modifying phrase modifies the subject of the next part of the sentence, which is the noun that appears *directly after the comma* (with the relevant articles, and in the second example, the adjective 'new').

Where, then, do people go wrong?

In a way, this issue is similar to the previously discussed 'mixed constructions': these sentences are problematic when the modifier does not clearly apply to the subject of the sentence. That is, the modifier 'dangles'. As with mixed constructions, it might be that parts of the sentence have been attached to each other, and all contribute to the same point, but do not work together grammatically.

The next two sentences are versions of the previous examples, rewritten incorrectly to demonstrate the 'dangling modifiers' problem:

> ✗ Feeling pressurised by declining ratings, the television network's advertising policy was adjusted by the executives.
>
> ✗ Originally developed to enhance efficiency in local health authorities, an important role emerged for the new database system, which would directly improve the experiences of the service users.

This issue can be quite difficult to detect. The two sentences above, if scanned (read quickly), might seem appropriate – particularly the second one.

As I've explained, when a sentence begins with a modifier, the modifier applies to the subject of the sentence, which will appear *at the beginning* of the second part of the sentence (after the comma). Applying this logic to the examples above reveals problems.

To test these sentences in your own work, take the first noun after the comma (the subject of the sentence), and place it *in front of* the modifier. Does your sentence make sense? Take a look at this step applied to the incorrect examples:

> × **Feeling pressurised by declining ratings, the television network's advertising policy** was adjusted by the executives.
>
> × The television network's advertising policy, feeling pressurised by declining ratings…

The bold text above includes the two parts I have reordered. Clearly, the 'advertising policy' cannot 'feel pressurised' by anything, given that it will be an inanimate text or legal document!

Doing the same exercise with the original, correct version of the sentence makes it clear that the *executives* (that is, people in charge of the television network) were 'feeling pressurised' – which makes perfect sense:

> ✓ **Feeling pressurised by declining ratings, the executives** changed the television network's advertising policy.
>
> ✓ The executives, feeling pressurised by declining ratings…

The second sentence, while longer, poses the same problem:

> × **Originally developed to enhance efficiency in local health authorities, an important role** emerged for the new database system, which would directly improve the experiences of the service users.
>
> × An important role, originally developed to enhance efficiency in local health authorities…

164

You can see that the *role* of the new database system cannot have been 'developed as a way to enhance efficiency'. That is what the new database system was developed for. Alternatively, the *role* of the database system might have been to enhance efficiency. It is very strange, however, to suggest that the role was developed to enhance efficiency.

The correct example makes things clearer:

> ✓ **Originally developed to enhance efficiency in local health authorities, the new database system** played an important role in directly improving the experiences of service users.
>
> ✓ The new database system, originally developed to enhance…

The key is to look out for any sentences you've written that begin with a modifier, separated from the main sentence by a comma. As you've seen, the modifier might contain a verb ending in 'ing', but not necessarily.

I'll show you one more incorrect example, and then a range of correct sentences written this way. This should give you a better idea of what they look like, and your skill in finding them will improve.

The following sentence, beginning with a dangling modifier, comes from an essay discussing the work and views of a historian:

> ✗ Writing about the later stages of the Cold War, the reader notices a more realist tone developing in Gottfried's analyses of, and conclusions surrounding, Western foreign policy.

Again, pair the modifying phrase with the *first noun* appearing in the second part of the sentence:

> ✗ The reader, writing about the later stages of the Cold War…

You can see here that a hurriedly written sentence, beginning with a dangling modifier, has ended up meaning something noticeably unusual. Read grammatically, the sentence suggests that Gottfried's *readers* have written about the Cold War. How can readers detect Gottfried's views in the text that they have, seemingly, written and *are reading*? The dangling modifier here has resulted in a sentence that defies logic!

165

To solve this problem, make sure that the point you need to make is clear to you. I know that in this example, *Gottfried* is doing the 'writing about the later stages of the Cold War'.

As such, I need to write a sentence that begins:

> ✓ Writing about the later stages of the Cold War, Gottfried…

Alternatively, I could change the modifier:

> ✓ Reading Gottfried's works on the later stages of the Cold War, the reader…

The problem with this second option is the repetition of 'read'; I could adjust further:

> ✓ Investigating Gottfried's conclusions about the later stages of the Cold War, the reader…

There are many possible options. For the sake of simplicity, I will complete a sentence based on the first solution: keeping 'Gottfried' as the subject of the sentence. Focusing on the historian I am writing about seems more appropriate than shifting my assignment's focus to the vague collection of 'readers'.

As always, when solving this problem, express your point simply and clearly. I might end up with something like this:

> ✓ Writing about the later stages of the Cold War, Gottfried develops a more realist tone as he analyses and draws conclusions from Western foreign policy.

In my improved example, I've made some changes beyond fixing the dangling modifier. I've emphasised verbs more than nouns to make the sentence seem more active: instead of the noun 'analysis', I've used the verb 'analyse'. Similarly, the noun 'conclusions surrounding' has become the verb 'draws conclusions from'.

Finally, rather than the 'realist tone' developing, I've used the more active formulation: 'Gottfried develops a more realist tone'. This keeps Gottfried as the subject, rather than the 'realist tone' itself, retaining the close focus on the historian I am analysing.

To conclude, here are several example sentences that *correctly* begin with modifiers:

✓ Having discussed the available treatment options, the physiotherapist and patient agreed upon a four-week regimen of various exercises.

✓ Subjected to increased academic interest over the past twenty years, project management, in its current range of forms, has been reinvigorated.

✓ Its script subsequently embellished by two co-authors, Cranston's fourth film marks a shift into less comedic territory.

Using 'It has been said that...'

As you've read in this book, and in the books on your reading lists, referencing appropriately and correctly, based on the research that you've done, is a *crucial* part of writing essays. In referencing, you have a system that enables you to incorporate the work of others into your own, and to do so in a way that is obvious and honest.

Because of this, if there is a point in your essay where your reader thinks you *could* or *should* have referenced, and you have not, you have a problem developing. Similarly, giving the vague impression that someone, at some point, *might* have written something that you're now going to use in your essay, is unacceptable. Referencing is clear, explicit and transparent.

The most common problematic phrases in this context aren't a problem in themselves. However, they pose a problem if they are not combined with adequate referencing, or if they are deliberately used to reinforce a point that is your own, and not anybody else's.

These common examples appear in sentences like the following:

✗ **It has been suggested that** the second episode of this popular television series represented the situation in Iraq.

✗ Although the stigma associated with AIDS sufferers has been considerably reduced, **it is said that** the illness still has negative connotations for many members of the public.

✗ Because the immediate practical benefits of high-cost, long-lasting physics research projects are often unclear, **the point has been raised that** substantial government investment in such projects might not have much support.

These sentences are grammatically correct, make clear points and are suitably academic in style. Yet, written as they are in an essay, they are going to cause huge problems.

Each one *immediately* raises a question in the reader's mind: '*Who* suggested that?'; '*Who* said that?'; '*Who* raised that point?'

There are several reasons for this mistake being made. One is that the author wants to make a point, but is (correctly) trying to avoid the first person in making it. To give it enough authority, a third-person statement like 'it has been suggested that' is chosen. Although the first person should be avoided, as you've learned, there is a deeper problem here: a problem with confidence. The next section of this chapter deals with this issue in particular.

The second reason, then, can be attributed to laziness or vagueness. As a student is frantically typing an essay mere hours from the deadline, they might remember a fantastic and important point from one of their lectures over the past year. Alternatively, they might think back to something that struck them from last night's pile of notes, journal articles, handouts and books...

In this scenario, the author *knows* that someone else has come up with an idea, or made a point (in the previous scenario, the author was making their own point), but can't remember who it is, or when it was made.

If this is the case, and you can't (or won't) find the information you need to reference a point, *you can't include it in your essay*. For some reason, sometimes people conclude that the phrase 'it has been suggested that...' is sufficient, and the reader will happily accept that a point has been made and has reinforcement behind it. This is not the case, however; that's exactly what referencing is for.

Another scenario involves the essay author trying, perhaps, to come up with some arguments that oppose the ones they have made in a previous section. They think of one, and then think something like, 'someone *must* have thought a similar thing at some point' and use the 'it has been said that...' or a similar phrase. In this situation, the writer knows they are making a point of their own, but is trying to give the impression it has been made by others.

There are two main options here: first, the student can include the point they are making, but as their own (again, the next section of this chapter is relevant here). They might decide, however, that this particular argument or point *needs* some reinforcement. They could, then, take a second approach: *deliberately* research the topic to see if this particular argument has been made.

Whether it has or not will affect what goes into the essay: if nobody has argued a particular point, the author could include it as their own. Alternatively, the author could include it as their own and detail why an argument might *not* have been made. If a point *has* been argued, the author has successfully carried out some deliberate, careful research that will probably have provided a range of material to write about. (Of course, if nobody has argued a particular point, the author may decide it is not worth making as a point of their own; this is fine, as long as the author thinks through the decision.)

Importantly, though, in either case, the author of the essay is using language, and using (or not using) referencing in an honest, clear way.

Key Point

Another phrase commonly used in this manner is 'it has been argued that...'

In conclusion, then, do not use phrases like 'it has been suggested that' unless you can prove that they are true – that is, reference them. To clarify, the following sentence, reworked from one of the above examples, would be appropriate (providing the references are accurate, of course!):

> ✓ Although the stigma associated with AIDS sufferers has been considerably reduced, **it is said that** the illness still has negative connotations for many members of the public (Wilkins, 2002; Shapiro, 2008).

If you cannot prove that the phrase is true, you as the writer need to decide whether to research the point (and then decide how or whether to include it, based on what you discover), to discard it, or to *confidently make the point your own.*

Using 'I think/I feel...'

Chapter 1 made clear the importance of being objective in academic writing. One convention that contributes to objectivity is avoiding the first person; academic writing should almost always be written in the third person.

Although following that convention will mean you're not in danger of making this mistake, I wanted to highlight it because it comes from a common problem with confidence in one's writing. A lack of confidence in our own work, especially as we are just starting our studies, is understandable. However, you don't want your writing to betray this.

169

> **Key Point**
>
> Note that an earlier chapter discussed 'hedging'. 'Hedging' means deliberately writing to show that you cannot be *sure* of a particular conclusion; that is, being deliberately cautious. Effective hedging actually demonstrates confidence in how solid your arguments are. As such, do not confuse 'hedging' with writing that lacks confidence.

There is a tendency among students, in assignments that otherwise follow the main academic conventions, to occasionally write a sentence like the one in bold, below. The extract is from an essay on the ethical and medical issues surrounding human medicine trials.

> ✗ Crocker and Ryan's work was pivotal in revealing the problem of human medical testing (1998). Although the subject had previously been raised in fiction, often to create tension or horror (Crichton, 1969; Cook, 1990), Crocker and Ryan presented an accessible, scholarly paper that highlighted the number of problematic trials that had been conducted. When a medical trial ended in the high-profile, widely reported organ failure of the patients (Ward, 2006; *Daily Mail*, 2006), yet more popular attention was focused on the subject. **I believe that the Western public as a whole, having been exposed to these sources, is comfortable enough with the medical trial as a *concept* to engage with it in a transparent, scientific debate.**

The extract is well-written, clear, appropriately referenced and academically acceptable – *except for the sentence in bold*.

One problem, on the surface, is the fact that phrases like 'I believe that...', 'I feel that...', 'In my opinion...' are not necessary in academic writing. Here is the same paragraph with the phrase removed:

> ✓ Crocker and Ryan's work was pivotal in revealing the problem of human medical testing (1998). Although the subject had previously been raised in fiction, often to create tension or horror (Crichton, 1969; Cook, 1990), Crocker and Ryan presented an accessible, scholarly paper that highlighted the number of problematic trials that had been conducted. When a medical trial ended in the high-profile, widely reported organ failure of the patients (Ward, 2006; *Daily Mail*, 2006), yet more popular attention was focused on the subject. **The Western public as a whole, having been exposed to these sources, is comfortable enough with the medical trial as a *concept* to engage with it in a transparent, scientific debate.**

Referencing has been used to demonstrate to the reader what has come from other sources. The last sentence, with no references, *must* be an argument that the author of the essay is making. The fact that it is clearly a conclusion drawing on the evidence in the previous sentences helps a great deal, but even if it were the first sentence in the paragraph, the reader would make the same assumption.

This idea came up in the referencing chapter: your work should always involve references that lead to your own conclusions and points. Unreferenced sentences will be read as your conclusions and points. There is no problem here.

Why, then, do these phrases ('I feel', 'I think', etc.) appear so often, even when students know not to use the first person 'I'?

The use of such phrases points to a lack of confidence.

This lack of confidence might be a *broad* one, very common when you are just starting out on a degree. This is often phrased as the question, 'Well, how can *I* include my own views among the points made by these *academics* and *experts*?' While it is understandable that you might have this worry, you need to get rid of it as quickly as you can. The reason that academic conventions, and referencing, and critical thinking, are so important is that they allow you to present your evidence, come to your own conclusions and get involved in the academic debate around a subject by giving all this to the reader.

Remove these kinds of phrases and work at making your writing effective, and your references appropriate and correct.

Alternatively, you might lack confidence *in this particular point*. If you have been happily writing your essay, and find that you have included one of these phrases – when you understand that you shouldn't – then actually examine the point you're making. Perhaps it does need a rethink.

Perhaps, instead, you need to 'hedge'; that is, be honest with the reader that your conclusion is tentative. This is *not* the same as telling the reader 'this point is my own; it doesn't belong to an expert, and you should be aware of that'. The reader knows this. Instead, you are saying, 'You're already aware that this point is mine, because it isn't referenced. I am making this point based on the evidence I have, which I've done my best to share with you, though I am being honest in that it *might be possible* to draw a different conclusion.'

Finally, then, here is the same example, but with some hedging language used instead of the 'I think' phrase:

> ✓ Crocker and Ryan's work was pivotal in revealing the problem of human medical testing (1998). Although the subject had previously been raised in fiction, often to create tension or horror (Crichton, 1969; Cook, 1990), Crocker and Ryan presented an accessible, scholarly paper that highlighted the number of problematic trials
>
> *(Continued)*

(Continued)

that had been conducted. When a medical trial ended in the high-profile, widely reported organ failure of the patients (Ward, 2006; *Daily Mail*, 2006), yet more popular attention was focused on the subject. The Western public as a whole, having been exposed to these sources, **seems** comfortable enough with the medical trial as a *concept* to, **perhaps**, engage with it in a transparent, scientific debate.

The broad point here is that unreferenced points will (correctly) be read as your own work.

Do not feel that you cannot include your own points in your work. Ensure that you are comfortable enough with each point you make, and that you have presented the evidence that led you to make the point. Finally, 'hedge' where necessary.

QUICK TIP: AFFECT OR EFFECT?

The words 'affect' and 'effect' are often confused. 'Affect' is a *verb*, while 'effect' is a *noun*. The following two sentences are correct:

- ✓ The treatment failed **to affect** the patient, whose condition worsened.
- ✓ The treatment had no **effect** on the patient, whose condition worsened.

Simply determine how you are using the word – whether it is an action (verb) or thing (noun). To remember this, remember that a verb is an action word. Action begins with 'a': 'affect' is the action.

Avoiding the word 'interesting'

This issue has nothing to do with grammar, or academic conventions. Based on my experience looking at essays, the word 'interesting' should be avoided. It seems to cause potential problems, rather than lead to effective writing.

Try not to describe anything as 'interesting'. One problem is that if you call something interesting, your reader might suspect that you don't consider the rest of your work interesting! It is also quite a weak and overused word that does not actually mean much. (Remember, too, the advice in this book about excessive and unnecessary description in general.)

Plenty of alternative words exist. In the box, I've demonstrated some sentences in which you might be tempted to include the word 'interesting', and then listed some other options:

> ✗ It is interesting that, in his final interview, Robertson did not mention the ongoing financial crisis, a topic that had permeated so powerfully into his latest poems.
>
> ✗ The two translations of this ancient Japanese text are almost identical, but the 1973 version, interestingly, uses the word 'right-mindedness' instead of 'righteousness'.

Alternatives include:

> ✓ It is worth noting … /It is worth pointing out…
>
> ✓ …notably…

Another different approach would be to shift the focus from pointing out that something is worth noting, to explaining *why* something is worth noting. You can link this to the larger point that you are making. In the box, you'll see one of the example sentences rewritten with this idea in mind:

> ✓ In his final interview, Robertson did not mention the ongoing financial crisis, a topic that had permeated so powerfully into his latest poems. This fact could support Willis' claim that the author was 'no longer so open about the intended meaning behind his work' (2010). The author himself once wrote that 'the reader plays the most important part of all' (Robertson, 2004). Alternatively, a more extreme conclusion, posited reluctantly by Browne (2010), suggests that Robertson's mental illnesses were, at this time, increasing in severity.

This seems rather a long extract – a whole paragraph now – when you consider that I only used it to replace calling something 'interesting'. However, if something is so noteworthy that you need to point it out, it probably is quite an important point to develop. In academic writing, you shouldn't point something out as being interesting in passing, or as a kind of 'add on'. Everything you write builds towards answering the essay question, or fulfilling the assignment brief. Logically, then, if you think you find something 'interesting', it is either interesting enough to merit full exploration, or not interesting enough to merit even a mention.

QUICK TIP: IMPORTANT IDEAS

The word 'interesting' appeared in my last sentence, which leads neatly on to this next tip. Using words like 'interesting' can cause a problem.

Here is another example:

'It is crucial to understand the context of NASA at the time of the Cold War.'

Don't label anything as 'important' or 'crucial' without explaining *why* it is so important. If you call a topic, idea, event or text important and don't tell the reader why, they will have certain worries and questions.

They might think that you have gathered from your research, or vaguely remember from a lecture, that an idea is important; you haven't, though, grasped the topic enough to understand the importance of it.

Alternatively, they might worry that they are missing out on key information, because you haven't explained the reasons that a topic is particularly important.

Poor presentation of tables and graphs

This issue really impacts on the impression an audience will have of your work, especially if it happens consistently throughout a longer piece of work (like a research project).

If you are going to include a graph or table which you have not produced, treat it like any other kind of reference (a quotation, a paraphrase, and so on). This means ensuring it is clear and readable, it is cited correctly in your text, and its relevance and importance is made obvious.

This last point means that not only do we use high-quality scans or images of the appropriate graphs (as opposed to poor-quality photocopies) and include not only a title (taken from the original source if possible), but also an appropriate and correct citation at the bottom right of the image (or foot-note the title, if that's more consistent with your referencing style). Finally, make sure that you explain the diagram's presence in your text, in the same way that you'd expand on or develop a quotation.

Doing this might range from including phrases as short and simple as, 'As diagram A, above, shows, the corporation's profits increased during the first half of the year...', to an entire paragraph explaining some of the key points or statistics visible in the diagram or graph. By doing this, you'll be showing that, as with your quoting and paraphrasing, you are using your research in a considered way, rather than just copying-and-pasting visual information and using that to make a point in, and by, itself.

Here is an example of a chart I have created, with the paragraph that follows it.

Number of students at Fordingham University over the past four academic years

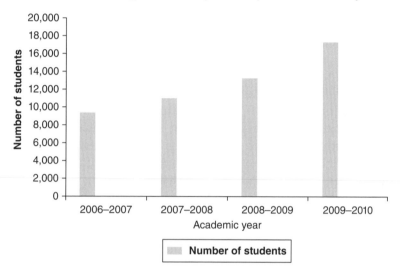

As the chart above shows, the number of students at Fordingham University has increased substantially each academic year since 2006. It is also apparent that the size of the increase has grown, particularly between academic years 2008–2009 and 2009–2010. This essay will examine the various factors that played a role in these increases.

QUICK TIP: PRACTISE OR PRACTICE?

'Practise' and 'practice' are often confused or misused. 'Practise' is a *verb*, while 'practice' is the *noun*. Knowing what function the word fulfils in a sentence will determine which spelling to use. To recall this, I remember that 'ice' is a noun, so 'practice', ending with the noun, is also a noun.

As such, these two example sentences are appropriate:

✓ Most journal articles published in the field of occupational therapy are written by established professionals who **have been practising** for years.

✓ **The practice** of occupational therapy is inseparable from the theory behind it.

(Continued)

175

(Continued)

Cases like this demonstrate how important it is to have an understanding of basic English grammar – if you weren't aware of the difference between a noun and a verb, you might never get this right!

Comma splicing

'Comma splicing' refers to separating grammatically complete sentences with a comma. This is one of the most common mistakes made in many kinds of writing, but its prevalence does not make it any more acceptable! While comma splicing might seem like a minor issue, it shares a danger common to some of the other mistakes discussed in this chapter: if it happens too frequently throughout your work or a section of it, your essay might end up practically unreadable, becoming a series of overlong sentences and unclear points glued together with commas.

Below is an example of a comma splice (so it is an incorrect sentence). Bear in mind that these sentences are cited in the Harvard style, but you could just as easily include a footnote, or number, depending on the referencing style you use. Once you have studied some examples, some ways around the problem can be discussed.

> ✗ De Tocqueville's investigation of American democracy (1835/1840) remains relevant today, many politics courses still list it as core reading.

If we separate this example into two parts, using the comma as our point of division, we get these:

> De Tocqueville's investigation of American democracy (1835/1840) remains relevant today

and

> many politics courses still list it as core reading

Read these sentences aloud, separately, and it should be fairly obvious that they are complete. This means that we cannot separate them just by using a comma. Here is a similar sentence that is not an example of comma splicing:

✓ Although De Tocqueville's investigation of American democracy (1835/1840) is nearly as old as America itself, many politics courses still list it as core reading.

Separating this in the same way gives us:

Although De Tocqueville's investigation of American democracy (1835/1840) is nearly as old as America itself

and

many politics courses still list it as core reading

The second part is identical, and it is still complete. The first part of the sentence, however, includes the conjunction 'although'. Read the first part of that sentence aloud and you will hear that something is quite obviously missing. That 'although' means that we need a second idea.

You may now have an idea about the rule to avoid comma splicing: at least one of the clauses, on either side of the comma, has to be incomplete when read by itself. This rule also applies to sentences made up of three or more clauses. Here is another comma splice:

✗ De Tocqueville investigated American democracy (1835/1840), his book is still widely considered relevant, the text is still listed as core reading on a wide range of politics courses.

This splits into three parts:

De Tocqueville investigated American democracy (1835/1840)

his book is still widely considered relevant

the text is still listed as core reading on a wide range of politics courses

Each of these, too, is complete; reading them aloud proves this immediately. We can ignore the citation, which might look different if another referencing style was being used. In any case, no referencing system would interfere with the grammatical sense of the sentence. Again, a slightly different example might not involve a comma splice:

> ✓ Nearly two hundred years after it was first published, De Tocqueville's (1835/1840) investigation of American democracy is still considered relevant, a fact emphasised by its inclusion as core reading in a wide range of politics courses.

Separating this into three parts gives us:

Nearly two hundred years after it was first published

De Tocqueville's (1835/1840) investigation of American democracy is still considered relevant

a fact emphasised by its inclusion as core reading on a wide range of politics courses

The second, or middle, clause is complete, and would work as a stand-alone sentence. The first, however, is a modifying clause that adds information (in this case, a rough date of publication) to another. As such, it does not make sense without the clause it is providing more detail about. As usual, reading this clause aloud will prove this point straight away. The same applies to the third clause. It is grammatically incomplete because it lacks a suitably formed verb, and if we wrote this as a sentence by itself, it might not be clear what 'a fact' refers to (here it is obvious because, again, the clause is modifying the previous one by telling us more about it).

This reaffirms the rule:

At least one of the clauses in a sentence that separates clauses with commas must be grammatically incomplete – that is, unable to stand as a sentence on its own.

Your sentence might have six clauses, and this rule still applies; in fact, as I have already mentioned, comma splicing becomes a much more problematic issue when it is used to link clause after clause, resulting in confusing, breathless paragraphs. Reading your work aloud is a very simple way of tracking this down. If you have any doubt as to whether a sentence is comma spliced, separate it into its constituent clauses in a separate word processor document, or on a separate sheet of paper. Double-check that at least one could not stand by itself.

Take a look at this example paragraph:

> ✗ De Tocqueville investigated American democracy (1835/1840), his book is still widely considered relevant, the text is still listed as core reading on a wide

range of politics courses. He wanted to see why republican representative democracy worked so well in the USA, he travelled round the states, he compared the American system to that of his native France, there are positive and negative aspects in what he found during this journey.

This paragraph 'sounds' very rushed and breathless, and it gives the impression that the author is stringing potentially valid, relevant points together without pausing to think about style or variety; the continued comma splicing actually makes the sentence very difficult to read. **This is important because** the presence of one paragraph like this in an essay means that there are likely to be others. As you can imagine, having to read whole sections of an essay written in this way would likely not have the best effect on your tutor's mood.

Identifying this very common problem is the first step; now we have to solve it.

Quite often the simple conjunctions 'and', 'but', 'then' and 'because' can be used, if they are appropriate.

For example, instead of the comma spliced sentence:

> ✗ De Tocqueville's investigation of American democracy was published in two volumes in 1835 and 1840, it is still relevant today.

We could use:

> ✓ De Tocqueville's investigation of American democracy was published in two volumes in 1835 and 1840 but it is still relevant today.

Here, 'but' is actually providing another layer of meaning – it is surprising or striking that De Tocqueville's book is still relevant, while, perhaps, most other books written as long ago as the 1800s might not be considered useful now.

Sometimes we can use a semi-colon. There is often confusion as to what a semi-colon actually does; as mentioned in Chapter 3, this is its most common purpose. It is used to join grammatically complete statements where the writer feels the link is so important that using two separate sentences would damage it (the sentence I've written above, 'Identifying this very common problem...' is actually an example of this). When it comes to rectifying comma-spliced sentences, using semi-colons instead of separate sentences, occasionally, is a good way of varying our writing style. See the example below.

> ✓ De Tocqueville does detail many negative points inherent in the American system of representative democracy; he discusses at some length what he sees as a lack of intellectual freedom in the country (1835/1840).

Finally, we can use separate sentences. This is often the simplest option, and it is better to write a paragraph of short separate sentences that make your points and express your ideas clearly than to write one filled with overlong, convoluted sentences and comma splicing.

Here, the writer has separated a comma-spliced sentence into three separate ones:

> ✓ One of De Tocqueville's aims was to compare and contrast the American system with that of France. His book had a lasting impact on intellectuals in both countries. It is also striking that many of the predictions he made about the future of American democracy would come true.

As you learn to develop your writing, you'll find that using a combination of the different solutions (joining some sentences together, using some semi-colons, splitting some spliced sentences into separate ones) will make your writing more varied and thus more interesting for the reader.

QUICK TIP: BEGINNING A SENTENCE WITH A NUMBER

There are various rules around writing numbers. These can vary from subject to subject; as you can imagine, different subjects use numbers to different extents.

Here is one rule that is the same across subjects: if you start a sentence with a number, you *must* write it, not use digits.

The following sentence would not be acceptable:

> ✗ 2 of the patients in the control group recovered at the same pace as those taking the experimental drug treatment.

Note that this rule applies even with large numbers. So, if you have a very large number you don't want to write in full, for example:

> Ten thousand, six hundred and sixty-seven is the total number of deaths resulting from extreme weather in the country, according to figures released by the government.

rearrange your sentence so it does not appear at the beginning, like so:

> The government has released figures that estimate the number of deaths resulting from extreme weather in the country at 10,667.

QUICK TIP: CONJUNCTIONS

Don't begin sentences with conjunctions (see the 'basic grammar' chapter for a list, but the common ones are: 'and',' but' and 'or'). Sometimes doing this is acceptable in other forms of writing, but it should be avoided in assignments.

However, be careful not to confuse conjunctions with *prepositions* (a much longer list, including: 'with', 'to', 'under', 'above', and many more).

Using 'of' instead of 'have'

This mistake is common in speech as well as writing; it probably appears in essays because the writers of the essays make the mistake when they talk.

In the second chapter, the verb as a grammatical device was defined and discussed. The third chapter examined the issue of verb 'tense'. Several tenses involve the word 'have' followed by an appropriate form of a particular verb.

The mistake being discussed here involves the word 'have' being incorrectly replaced by 'of'. 'Of' is not a verb, and as such, does not appropriately create a certain tense when it is paired with a verb. Here are some examples of correct usage:

✓ Although the legislation was only passed two years ago, its results, judging by rising grades in Indian primary schools, **have been** encouraging.

✓ Until the opening of the Soviet archives, commentators, politicians, historians and journalists could (and many did) warn about the expansionist nature of the Communist regime, but could **not have *known*** just how expansionist the empire was.

(Continued)

(Continued)

✓ Walker was approached by a major film studio interested in adapting his first novel, a full thirty years after the events of the novel are meant to **have taken place.** Walker turned the studio down because they insisted on updating the setting which would **'have been** disastrous' (Walker, 1986, p340).

The following versions of these sentences, then, would be incorrect (but this mistake is so common I would not be surprised if I saw them):

✗ Until the opening of the Soviet archives, commentators, politicians, historians and journalists could (and many did) warn about the expansionist nature of the Communist regime, but could **not of *known*** just how expansionist the empire was.

✗ Walker was approached by a major film studio interested in adapting his first novel, a full thirty years after the events of the novel are meant to **of taken place.** Walker turned the studio down because they insisted on updating the setting which would **'have been** disastrous' (Walker, 1986, p340).

Note that in the final example, the second use of 'have been' is a *direct quote*, which the essay author could not change. In a way, this would act as a clue to the other mistake!

The most common formation of this mistake seems to be 'would have' and 'could have' (or the negative equivalents 'would not have' or 'could not have') being incorrectly written 'would of' and 'could of'.

'Of' is a preposition that labels a specific relationship between one noun and another; this relationship is often possessive, as it is in the following example:

✓ The effects **of** the excesses of Senators like Joe McCarthy and the House Un-American Activities Committee reverberated through American politics, massively straining public confidence in it, for decades. Additionally, as a consequence **of** the later Watergate scandal, faith in the federal government would drop even more.

As you can see, the phrase 'would of', for example, has nothing to do with the specific meaning of the word 'of', nor is it a correct verb form.

Use your word processor's find tool to track down all your uses of the word 'of'. (There is another reason to do this, explained in a separate subsection.) Check that it has been used correctly, and is never connected to the verbs 'would', 'could', 'should' or 'will', in particular.

If you take care to write your verbs correctly, and think through the appropriate tenses for your sentences, as discussed in Chapter 3, you should not notice this problem at all.

QUICK TIP: OVERLONG/CONVOLUTED SENTENCES

This has already been mentioned, but is such a common mistake that I wanted to highlight it again in this section.

Briefly: if reading a sentence aloud leaves you breathless, it's too long! Simply break it down into manageable chunks, even if this occasionally leads to some repetition. Similarly, if you have difficulty checking that verbs (for example) agree with the appropriate nouns, because they are so far apart, you might have a problem.

The word 'of' and possessive replacements

The 'possessive', as well as the letter 's' and the apostrophe that goes with it, were discussed in Chapter 3.

Although this is not a mistake, as such, it's worth knowing that in *most* cases, the word 'of' is used to represent the possessive. It can often, therefore, be replaced by the simpler possessive apostrophe and 's'.

Here are some examples that show this replacement in action:

The aim of the study was to investigate the effects of long-term steroid abuse by males between the ages of 19 and 27.

The study's aim was to investigate the effects of long-term steroid abuse by males between the ages of 19 and 27.

One of the objectives **the designers of the game** set out to achieve, starting with **the style of the interface**, was creating a 'truly immersive experience' (Halshaw, 2006, p23).

One of the objectives **the game's designers** set out to achieve, starting with **the interface's style**, was creating a 'truly immersive experience' (Halshaw, 2006, p23).

(Continued)

> *(Continued)*
>
> During the early stages of the primary campaign, it was clearly **the intention of Governor Clinton** to prove that he was **a different kind of Democrat**. **The structure of his campaign operation** allowed him to ensure this theme was reinforced at every level.
>
> During the early stages of the primary campaign, it was clearly **Governor Clinton's intention** to prove that he was **a different kind of Democrat**. **His campaign operation's structure** allowed him to ensure this theme was reinforced at every level.

In the last example, one use of the word 'of' ('a different kind of Democrat') has not been changed. The phrase 'a Democrat's different kind' does not make sense. This highlights the fact that it's always up to you as the author to choose whether to make this substitution. Sometimes, as in this example, the replacement doesn't make sense.

In other cases, using the possessive 's' might sound or read strangely; if in doubt, leave the original 'of' in the sentence.

Below are some phrases in which you need to keep the word 'of'. These are just some examples; again, using 'of' is not incorrect. The possessive can be simpler, but cannot always be used instead.

> Part of the problem…
>
> Several of the…
>
> Many of the…
>
> Some of the…
>
> One of the important facts from the…

Finally, I've included a sentence in which I *could* use the possessive, but would choose not to, because the resulting sentence seems a bit strange to me. Rather than leave a sentence that bothers me in my essay, I've left it as it is.

> The shift of the focus in the play from the imprisoned criminals to their guards is a subtle one.

A version with the possessive replaced would look like this:

> The focus' shift in the play from the imprisoned criminals to their guards is a subtle one.

The phrase 'focus' shift' looks odd, and sounds odd when read aloud. It seems a bit forced and awkward. As such, this possibility to replace 'of' with the simple possessive should be seen as one potential technique available to you when writing. Sometimes it will help streamline your writing. At other times it should not be used.

'Putting things off'

An essay's introduction, or the introductory parts of chapters in a longer assignment, usually does a number of things. The introduction explains the context of a topic, outlines the reader's argument and, crucially, summarises what the essay is going to investigate.

The last of these, explaining the various steps an assignment will take, naturally involves sentences and paragraphs that tell the reader that something *will* be discussed, rather than actually discussing the particular something *now*.

This is appropriate, and readers will expect your introduction to do this. However, when the same phenomenon happens later in a piece of work, it can cause an unusual problem.

Sometimes, in essays, students give the impression of 'putting things off', by explaining what is going to appear in a piece of work, instead of just raising the topic.

Below, you'll see an example of this:

> ✗ Before discussing the present state of Marxist theory, a definition of Marxism is necessary.

While there is nothing grammatically wrong with this sentence, it is a waste of words that could be put to better use. The author should simply provide the 'necessary' definition, like so:

> ✓ Marxism can be defined as…

After a definition has been provided, the author can go on to discuss 'the present state of Marxist theory'.

The following example is similarly problematic:

> ✗ At this point, some information about the context of the NASA space programme at the time is needed.

The phrase 'at this point' means *now*. If some information is needed *now*, provide it now! The author could simply write a clear, simple paragraph detailing the context of the space programme:

> ✓ At the time, the NASA space programme was a complex set of projects, each with distinct aims, involved individuals, and budgets.

This might strike you as a strange issue, but you'd be surprised how commonly it appears in assignments. After all, nobody *deliberately* decides to delay discussion unnecessarily.

This is just a theory of my own, but I think this happens because, to an author trying to make their work seem 'academic', highlighting the fact that you are about to provide an important definition can seem formal, somehow.

Take another look at the example about Marxism. I get the impression that a student, in writing this sentence, might think the sentence says something like this: 'I am discussing a very important and academic topic, and I understand that it's very important to define key terms in essays, so I am going to prove that I think this way by telling the reader I'm about to do so.'

The problem with this approach, of course, is that the student is forgetting that simply defining the 'important and academic topic' proves the same thing to the reader. In fact, it proves it in a simpler, more effective way.

Again, that is my tentative explanation for why this issue appears; remember, don't try to be any more formal than necessary. This applies to both the formality of writing style, as well as the over-formal approach of unnecessarily 'building up' to a grand topic, which actually just appears like you are delaying the inevitable.

Bear in mind that if you *do* need to explain why a certain point needs to be made before another one, then it's appropriate to do so. That is, if you are aware that something needs to be delayed, and *can explain why*, then explain it. This, in fact, would be considered signposting. Consider this revised version of the previous example:

✓ In order to understand the part that the NASA space programme played in America's Cold War strategy, it is crucial to understand the context of NASA at the time.

If I were to take out the reason for delaying a discussion, I'd be left with a sentence more like the earlier, problematic ones:

✗ It is crucial to understand the context of NASA at the time of the Cold War.

The second version, and the earlier sentences, are examples of an unnecessary kind of signposting: 'I need to give you this important information now. Here is the important information.'

The first version of the NASA sentence, however, makes clear *why* the information is important: 'I need to give you this information *because it helps you understand* what comes next.'

To summarise: do not delay making a point, unless you can explain why you need to. If it is worth writing, it is worth writing now!

8

Proofreading Effectively

While this chapter summarises some ideas the book has already discussed, it focuses on a key part of writing that students often neglect. This can result in losing marks unnecessarily.

Effective proofreading and editing are both linked to effective planning and time management. Any plan for writing an assignment, or for dividing up the time you're going to spend on an assignment, should take editing and proof-reading stages into account. Because of the nature of this book, I focus on the actual word-by-word practice of editing and proofreading effectively. You will find many academic skills books have excellent sections on time management and planning.

What is 'proofreading'? What is 'editing'? Are they different things?

As I've done throughout this book, I'll provide my own basic definitions.

'Editing' means making any changes to work you've already done, at any point in the writing process. By my definition, editing could include any of the following examples: rewriting a paragraph; removing a sentence; inserting references; redrafting a whole section.

'Proofreading' is a specific type of editing. Proofreading is less about changing work you've already done, and more about ensuring that what you *have* done is correct. Proof-reading, defined like this, could include: making sure sentences are grammatically correct and punctuated properly; double-checking your use of capital letters and apostro-phes; making sure that your referencing is formatted correctly; fixing any typos (incorrectly typed words) or problems with missing words.

Another way of putting this is that editing can be seen as a broader exercise, in which you might change the actual content or meaning of your essay, or make structural changes to help the reader make better sense of your argument.

Proofreading is more like 'tidying up' an assignment to make sure that it is 'correct' and ready for submission. Although simple things like moving apostrophes *can* inadvertently change the meaning of a sentence, the *aim* of proofreading is not to actually change the substance of an essay. It is to present existing substance correctly.

In some ways, it does not matter what the stages of the writing process are called, as long as they happen. Using my definitions, however, you realise that large parts of this book are about editing. I have written extensively about how to change your writing to make it better. As your writing develops, you'll make the kinds of decisions I recommend as you are writing. Of course, you'll still constantly revisit and redraft your text.

This means that many of the ideas in this book up to this point could be seen as part of the editing process. You *should* often re-read what you've written, and should always be prepared to make changes as you do so.

I have explained the difference between proofreading and editing so I can now make clear what this chapter intends to do: provide advice on how to effectively 'tidy up' your work before handing it in for marking.

Because of the nature of proofreading, the focus here is not on broad changes to pieces of work but on making sure that the work is presented in a high quality way that is ready to be marked.

What follows is a sequence of tips, recommendations, suggestions and techniques to help you make the most of the proofreading you do.

Distance yourself from your work

You may have spent hours, days, weeks or even months on an essay, reading and writing about a particular topic. You've redrafted parts of your work, likely many times, and generally worked so hard on this particular assignment that you could probably recite most of it from memory.

Quite naturally, you get *attached* to what you've written. By this I don't just mean that you end up memorising a lot of your work, though this does happen, but as you draft and redraft, you rightly develop a deep sense of pride in your writing. Even if you think the assignment is going badly, and you don't feel 'pride' as such, you will still feel this attachment.

This is normal and to be expected. In many ways it is a good thing: if you're not attached to what you're writing, you won't care about it. This will show in the quality (or lack of quality!) of your writing.

This attachment makes proofreading more difficult, though. Because you are so familiar with what you've written, it becomes much harder to spot the mistakes on your pages. You are so used to seeing these particular sentences in this particular order, that your brain misses misplaced apostrophes and missing words.

This is a danger even if you read through your work several times. As you read, your brain 'fills in the blanks' and you overlook mistakes that might be obvious to someone else reading your work for the first time.

When I recommend 'distancing' yourself from your piece of work, I mean trying to proofread objectively. Read each word as it is on the page, and try not to think about the actual content you've spent so much time on. Try and look at your writing neutrally. Let your eyes see what *is* there instead of your brain 'sensing' what *should* be there, or what you *think* is there.

Establishing this kind of 'neutral' frame of mind is vital when proof-reading your work. Some of the tips below will help you achieve this in a practical way.

Ultimately, though, this is a state of mind. In this sense it is similar to the idea of attaining conciseness in our writing. There are practical techniques to use to improve your work.

As you sit down to proofread one final time, physically shake your head to get rid of the enthusiasm you've worked up for the topic, and the arguments you've carefully constructed. Have the confidence to accept that you have worked hard on this assignment, and now you need to put aside that hard work (only temporarily!) so you can concentrate on each word on each page. That way, you'll spot all the mistakes you may have ended up making – and you can remove them.

Proofread more than once

It is vital you read through your whole piece of work when it is finished. However, you can (and should) proofread more than just this once. You can use the techniques outlined in this chapter *as you write* a piece of work – every 1000 words, for example, or after every subsection. This way, proof-reading becomes an 'iterative' process. This means that the process is repeated. Each repetition builds on and enhances what has happened previously.

Bear in mind, though, proofreading several times means you get more familiar with the work you've written, in the way mentioned above. Overall, it's worth the risk; getting more attached to your work (as long as your final proofreading exercise is as objective as possible – try some of the other tech-niques in this chapter) is better than only proofreading once.

Leave more time than you think you need

Be prepared to leave a generous amount of time for proofreading your finished piece of work. Giving yourself more time will, obviously, allow you to proofread carefully. You'll find it less stressful and you'll make corrections more calmly.

There is another benefit: if you've given yourself plenty of time to proofread, and you notice a larger problem, you have more time to resolve it. If you have left proofreading to the last minute, you're more likely to panic and make poor choices. Alternatively, you might decide you just don't have the time to make the changes, and ignore what you've discovered. Neither is ideal.

Read your work aloud

This technique has been repeatedly recommended throughout the book. Don't underestimate how useful it can be. Reading your work aloud is one of the best ways of finding the little mistakes your eyes don't 'see'. Make sure you carefully read what is on the page. Again, don't try and make this task quicker by reading what you remember, or what you *think* you've written.

You will hear immediately if you have misspelled a word (and try to read the misspelled version aloud); repeated a word; dropped a letter; left a sentence incomplete; and so on. Additionally, over-long, confusing sentences are more likely to make you run out of breath, or stumble. This means you'll notice them.

If you're working in groups, have someone else read your work. Hearing someone else read your work can really help establish the distance you're aiming for. Then you can be more objective about evaluating and editing your work. Go back and re-read the 'Common mistakes' chapter in this book. Think about how many of them are easier to spot if they are read aloud. Not every single one, of course, but certainly many of them.

Read from your last sentence back

I used to phrase this technique by saying to students, 'read your work backwards'. I quickly realised that this was often misunderstood, and I can see why!

What I actually mean is this: read your individual sentences in the correct order, but begin reading with the last sentence. Read each previous sentence until you finish proofreading on the first one in the essay. If this is too confusing, you can do it with complete paragraphs – read the last paragraph of the essay, then the one before it, then the previous one again, and so on.

This method might take some time. Doing this is another way of forcing yourself to focus on the words you've written without getting lost in the meaning of your work. It will make the argument in your essay almost unintelligible (impossible to understand), and force you to concentrate sentence-by-sentence. Because of this, reading from the last sentence backwards is one of the last things you should do before you hand your assignment in.

Even if you spot, say, four typing errors doing this, you're still removing mistakes that would give your readers the impression that you hadn't taken the time to check your essay properly. As such, this method can seem quite tedious but is often worth the trouble.

Use technology but don't rely on it

Increasingly, technology-based tools can be used to help you as you write. At a basic level, for example, most word processors will have some kind of grammar/spell-checking tool. Many online tools do similar things. Your university might provide access to certain kinds of software to help you plan your work – mind-mapping tools, for example.

It is important to bear in mind that using technology effectively and relying on technology are very different things; Kelly summarises this excellently:

WHAT YOUR TUTORS SAY

'Don't rely on the spelling and grammar check in your word processor.' – Kelly, Sport Psychology lecturer

---

Kelly's point is crucial. The important verb in her advice is 'rely'. Word processors, like all technology, can provide incredible help if used correctly. However, *relying* on them, or not putting any thought into how you use them, can be unhelpful. If you rely on these tools, in the absence of understanding basic principles of academic writing and grammar, you are more likely to end up *damaging* your work.

Key Point

I can give a relevant example from my own teaching here. A student came to me with an essay that used some very strange vocabulary. This seemed to get more problematic as the work went on. Eventually the sentences were so odd they didn't make sense at all.

Many of the sentences, which actually had quite simple meanings, were filled with archaic words (words that are not used in modern English), rare words and formal phrases.

The reason was that the student had been using the thesaurus tool to 'vary her vocabulary'. Nearly every time she had to write a word she'd used before, she put it into the thesaurus and picked the next alternative word available. This resulted in writing that got more bizarre as she pushed the thesaurus to its limits!

This is an example of good intentions (trying to introduce variety into her writing) brought down by relying on the technology instead of using it for help. This example also reinforces a point I've repeated in this book: *try* and write simply. Don't force your writing away from simplicity!

In this book, I've recommended the 'find' tool many times. This only works if you know what you are trying to find. That's why, whenever I have recommended the tool, I have also given guidance as to what to search for.

Grammar-checkers in word processors can be very useful. They can also be wrong. If you don't have a decent idea of the rules of grammar and punctuation, you won't know when to ignore or adapt what a grammar-checking tool advises you to do.

Spell-checking tools are more often correct. They still should be used with caution. If you've obviously misspelled a word, they will usually recommend the correct version. They might, however, recommend several words; you will have to choose the right one. If you have typed a completely incorrect version of a word, your computer might think you're trying to type something completely different. Its recommendations might then be wrong.

The simpler your writing is, the less likely these problems are. If your subject or topic involves the use of technical terms or subject-related jargon, then type them very carefully. As you find them in your reading, especially if they come up a lot, make sure you *know* how to spell them. Identify words you'll often need to use but worry you'll struggle with, and take the time to learn them.

Note that reading your work aloud won't differentiate between words that have been confused and *sound* the same: 'piece' and 'peace' are different things, but they sound the same.

Be ruthless

The attachment we all feel towards what we've written will develop whether our work is good or 'bad' (though sometimes we feel attached to a piece of work, because we're proud of how good it is).

We've discussed how powerful this attachment can be. Trying to distance ourselves from our work is one important part of proofreading. Another piece of advice I have for you to deal with this is: be ruthless.

By 'ruthless', I mean willing to make major changes to your work when you decide they are necessary. If a paragraph is not working, for example, make a note of the key point you need to make, and don't spend a long time hesitating – chop the paragraph out. Rework or rewrite it, making the key point in a way that works.

Again, I can provide an example from my own writing. An early draft of this paragraph had an additional paragraph before this one. I decided it was repeating points I'd already made in this chapter. This was especially ironic given the topic of this section. Rather than hesitating, or making small changes, I gritted my teeth and deleted the entire paragraph.

Doing this becomes easier the more you write. Additionally, as you get more used to what is expected of you in academic writing, you'll edit your work more ruthlessly.

Be prepared to remove whole paragraphs if you realise you can't make the case for them being in the essay. Similarly, if you are slightly unsure as to whether you've used a word correctly, and can't find a definite answer – it is better to go for something simpler that you *know* makes sense.

Being 'ruthless' is a hard skill to teach. It is another way of thinking; another aspect of the state of mind we need to be in to edit and proofread our assignments effectively.

As you develop your understanding of what your tutors expect from your assignments, you'll find it easier to delete or edit work based on how effective the extracts are as *academic writing*, not based on how much or how little time you've spent on a section.

Being reluctant to rewrite a section you've spent a long time on, even if you know it isn't your best work, is a more common way of thinking in the early stages of your development as a writer.

This all ties in with many other things I have discussed – quite often, students complain that word counts are too short. Yes – you are being assessed on making key points succinctly. This *is* difficult.

Academics must do this when they write articles for journals. So do people working in business, when they give presentations or reports to stakeholders. Many fields and many jobs will require that you make convincing arguments that are to-the-point.

This is a fact of life, and learning to be ruthless and remove anything that does not directly contribute to an answer takes a long time. The main point I am making here is: be prepared to start learning that.

I'll leave it to Simon to offer some advice on ruthlessness:

WHAT YOUR TUTORS SAY

'If you get stuck, it is often better to throw away old versions and write them from scratch. It never takes as long as you think, and always ends up with better results.' – Simon, Computing lecturer

---

Simon's quote highlights a potential benefit of rewriting portions of your essays: you might end up with much better work.

Proofread for *you*...

By 'proofread for you' I mean several things.

The first is that you should try and learn what issues affect your work most. Then you can actively seek to address them during proofreading.

It's easy to forget that sometimes we repeat the same mistakes. Additionally, we all have a writing style, and can develop certain habits that might be hard to get rid of. As you write and edit your work, and look for some of the issues you've learned about, *try and keep an eye on trends*. By 'trends', I mean similar sorts of issues coming up over and over. Some of these trends will be easy to spot. If you *keep* misusing apostrophes, you know to prioritise double-checking your apostrophes when you proofread. You can also prioritise addressing the issue in terms of your own grammatical knowledge.

It might be more difficult to work out why you seem to write so many complicated sentences – but try and investigate. Perhaps you are overusing commas and just sticking sentences together?

Learning what issues keep arising in your writing is worthwhile for two reasons. You'll know what to prioritise for double-checking when you edit and proofread. You'll also know what to be careful of *as* you write each essay draft.

Key Point

Developing your academic writing can get more daunting when you realise how many different factors there are to consider, and how many aspects of writing to improve.

(Continued)

(Continued)

To make it easier, try to prioritise what you next read up on, or revise, or deliberately set about improving. For example, you might say to yourself: 'I am going to focus on my use of references in paragraphs.'

This will take a lot of the stress and fear out of improving your work. I'm sometimes surprised by how easily this idea is forgotten. As you edit and proofread, look for themes and trends. Make lists. Prioritise issues.

Imagine that you have identified misused apostrophes as an issue to solve. Think about how good you will feel when your next essay comes back with none of them. By having clear objectives you will know when you are making real progress.

The second suggestion I mean by 'proofread for you' is to learn how to make your proofreading time as efficient as it can be.

As well as proofreading 'for you' by trying to be aware of things *you* need to look out for, you should also proofread in a way that is effective for you. This could mean many things.

If you find it difficult to proofread by reading your own work aloud but learn that your proofreading is incredibly effective when you listen to someone *else* reading your work – try and do it that way whenever possible. Bribe your friends! Offer to read their work, perhaps.

Different people have different preferences when it comes to typing as opposed to writing by hand. Your various tutors might mark your work in different ways. Don't force yourself to proofread in a way that feels uncomfortable. If you like to have paper in front of you to scribble notes on, then print out your latest essay draft. Make your changes, and then type them up. If you find it easier to use a keyboard and screen, don't waste time by trying to do things on paper.

A lot of this advice comes down to common sense, but it is surprising how often we can all leave common sense behind when we are writing assignments.

Key Point

I have identified the techniques that help *me* proofread most effectively.

This is how I usually edit, rewrite and proofread (it might vary depending on the length of what I'm writing): I will type a draft of a section of work, like a chapter of this book. When I'm happy that the draft is finished and it's time to edit, I print the chapter. I then make changes using a red pen. As I type my changes up, I usually find I develop *more* ideas that I type without having written them down in red.

I include this here just to show you an example of a particular process that I find effective. I find it difficult to keep track of changes to writing on a screen, and prefer to work with actual paper, before retyping.

It works for me – so I carry on doing it this way!

To sum up, it's important to remember that although you have to follow conventions in your essays, referencing rules and English grammar rules, it doesn't matter how you actually end up with a finished essay. (That is, as long as it's your own work, of course.) I once saw a student who had to listen to particular music every time she proofread her assignments. Other people need complete silence. Find out what works for you, and do it that way.

Key Point

When prioritising your proofreading, use the feedback you've been given by your tutors for previous pieces of work, or spoken feedback they've given during seminars or conversations with them. Anything a tutor writes down or tells you about your work is potentially useful. Sometimes students only focus on the written feedback they receive when they get a final mark back for an assignment. Your tutors will often have more feedback that they'll give to you and your peers in various ways.

This doesn't just apply to proofreading, but writing as a whole. If one of your lecturers keeps telling you that you need to brush up on your grammar, make sure you pay attention!

... And keep things in context

Although I've suggested you leave plenty of time for proofreading, in the real world, you might often have several deadlines looming. You'll also have plenty of other reading and studying to get on with. Of course you will have to make choices as to how you manage your time.

I have highlighted the importance of prioritising – looking for the issues you know you need to look for. I would add that it is easy to look for fairly minor issues to put off addressing larger ones. It is human nature to tackle the smaller or easier jobs to avoid the ones you worry will be difficult.

This, then, is a reminder to keep things in context. Realistically, you are not going to lose a huge amount of marks for forgetting one capital letter at the start of an author's surname. You *are* going to lose marks if your sentences change tense repeatedly throughout every paragraph you write.

In an ideal world, neither would happen. However, if you know or suspect you have a problem with a larger, more damaging issue like getting sentence structure confused, it is better to tackle that instead of combing your work for spelling errors. Yes, this might be a more daunting and tiring task, but you will benefit in the end.

Put simply: when you're prioritising, try and focus on the bigger issues first. This will become easier as you learn more about yourself as a writer. Then you will develop an awareness of what the bigger issues might be.

Do your own proofreading

Students often approach me to ask if anyone at the university will proofread their work for them, or if I can recommend any proofreading services online.

Most universities do not offer proofreading services. Academic skills or study skills services and tutors, like me, won't proofread assignments. We might give general guidance on extracts from essays (my experience of doing this is where much of the material in this book comes from).

There is a proofreading industry, though. Publishers might employ proof-readers. Magazines and newspapers also need this kind of service. So why won't I proofread the work of students who come to me? (Aside from the fact that I simply don't have the time.) Why do I recommend that you do your own proofreading?

The answer is simple. In the context of academic writing, proofreading is a very important skill to learn. Nobody can teach you how to do it, though you can be given guidance, as this chapter has tried to do. If you don't get used to proofreading your own work yourself, you'll never be able to fully develop your writing.

I've suggested above that you prioritise issues that come up in your work; you won't know what they are unless you proofread your work yourself. Proofreading teaches you a lot about your own writing – you won't learn these things if you don't go through the process yourself.

There's also the element of the future: if, as part of your job, you have to write reports or do other formal writing, or, as an academic, do more aca-demic writing, you'll be expected to produce high-quality work with no mis-takes. If you're not used to proofreading, you won't have the skills to do it effectively; it is like any other skill in this respect.

Index

WRITING FOR ACADEMIC SUCCESS

Second Edition

Gail Craswell *Australian National University, Canberra* and **Megan Poore** *University of Canberra*

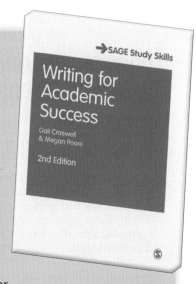

Writing for Academic Success is a vital practical guide for any postgraduate student. If you seek to manage your writing effectively, reduce stress, and improve your confidence and efficiency, this book is for you. The authors show you how to acquire communicative rigor in research essays, reports, book and article reviews, exam papers, research proposals, and literature reviews, through to thesis writing, posters and papers for presentation and publication.

This second edition has been fully revised to reflect the online learning explosion. The authors provide insightful new material about how to work productively in different online contexts such as with blogs and wikis, setting up an e-portfolio, and raising an online profile. They also set out a focused guide to issues unique to digital communication, and working with and across different media and technologies.

The book includes advice on common writing concerns, cross-cultural and inter-disciplinary practices, a list of helpful words and phrases, and subject-specific examples of writing ranging from economics to philosophy to medicine. **Writing for Academic Success** is essential for graduate students both in taught courses and conducting research, and is also very useful for upper-level undergraduates.

Visit **www.sagepub.co.uk/studyskills.sp** for free downloads, special offers and more!

SAGE STUDY SKILLS SERIES
2011 • 264 pages
Cloth 978-0-85702-927-0) • £65.00
Paper 978-0-85702-928-7) • £22.99

ALSO FROM SAGE